Election Politics and the Mass Press in Long Edwardian Britain

This book explores the ways in which the emergence of the 'new' daily mass press of the late-nineteenth and early-twentieth centuries represented a hugely significant period in histories of both the British press and the British political system.

Drawing on a parallel analysis of election-time newspaper content and archived political correspondence, the author argues that the 'new dailies' were a welcome and vibrant addition to the mass political culture that existed in Britain prior to World War I. Chapters explore the ways in which the three 'new dailies' – Mail, Express, and Mirror – represented political news during the four general elections of the period; how their content intersected with, and became a part of, the mass consumer culture of pre-Great War Britain; and the differing ways political parties reacted to this new press, and what those reactions said about broader political attitudes towards the worth of 'mass' political communication.

This book will be of interest to students and scholars of media history, British popular politics, journalism history, and media studies.

Christopher Shoop-Worrall is a Lecturer in Media and Journalism at UCFB Etihad Campus and an Early Career Member of the Royal Historical Society.

Routledge Focus on Journalism Studies

For more information about this series, please visit: https://www.routledge.com

Election Politics and the Mass Press in Long Edwardian Britain

Christopher Shoop-Worrall

Routledge
Taylor & Francis Group

LONDON AND NEW YORK

First published 2022
by Routledge
4 Park Square, Milton Park, Abingdon, Oxon OX14 4RN

and by Routledge
605 Third Avenue, New York, NY 10158

Routledge is an imprint of the Taylor & Francis Group, an informa business

© 2022 Christopher Shoop-Worrall

The right of Christopher Shoop-Worrall to be identified as author of this work has been asserted in accordance with sections 77 and 78 of the Copyright, Designs and Patents Act 1988.

British Library Cataloguing-in-Publication Data
A catalogue record for this book is available from the British Library

Library of Congress Cataloging-in-Publication Data
A catalog record has been requested for this book

ISBN: 978-1-032-18231-5 (hbk)
ISBN: 978-1-032-18380-0 (pbk)
ISBN: 978-1-003-25426-3 (ebk)

DOI: 10.4324/9781003254263

Typeset in Times New Roman
by codeMantra

Contents

Acknowledgements

Practically, the research undertaken for this book could not have happened without the invaluable guidance and patience of the staff at the archives accessed throughout the years of this project. Thanks goes to the staff at the People's History Museum in Manchester, the Working Class Movement Library in Salford, the University of Oxford's Bodleian Library (especially Jeremy McIlwaine), the Bishopsgate Institute, the British Library, the archives within the London School of Economics, and Annie Pinder at the Parliamentary Archives in Westminster. A debt is also owed to the organisations and conferences at which aspects of this book were presented, particularly the Newspaper and Periodical History Forum of Ireland (NPHFI) and the rigour and kindness of its members. A huge thank you as well to Suzanne Richardson and Tanushree Baijal at Routledge, for their invaluable editorial skill in turning my doctoral research into this book.

A huge debt is owed to people at two institutions. The University of Sheffield's Centre for the Study of Journalism and History was the perfect PhD home. Particular thanks to Professors Martin Conboy and Adrian Bingham: thank you for having faith in me and this research, and for being such strong, considerate supervisors. To my friends and colleagues at UCFB: thank you for being so welcoming, and for your continuance support of my work.

To my parents and two brothers: thank you for the lifetime of support.

Finally, to my wife and closet friend: thank you for being, simply, the best.

1 Introduction

(I am) generally <u>not</u> a politician... a teetotaller, anti-vaccinationist, or a vegetarian, or any sort of crank... industrious... casual and intermittent interest in football matches and race meetings... I like the theatre and the music hall – the latter, perhaps the more... sympathetic, but not sentimental... England for the English, a happy England populated by prosperous Englishman...
I am the Man in the Street.[1]

Published on the first day of the 1906 general election campaign, a news article from page four of the *Daily Express* claimed to be written from the perspective of the 'man in the street'. This individual claimed to be 'the Man who can Control our Destinies'. He was the person from whom all political parties would be seeking a vote. This same man in the street was very similar to the individual, according to the dismissive comments of the then Prime Minister and Conservative leader Lord Salisbury, who ran and read the *Daily Mail* from its inception in May 1896: 'a newspaper produced by office boys for office boys'.[2] Salisbury's negativity ignored the importance of who the *Mail,* by his own admission, was particularly appealing to. All three of the new dailies – the *Express, Mail,* and the *Mirror* – built their successes throughout the Long Edwardian[3] period upon their shared ability to speak to the office-working man in the street, and millions of other lower-middle- and upper-working-class[4] British citizens whose lives resonated with the *Express's* short biography.[5]

This book identifies the significance of the Long Edwardian period within histories of both the British press and the British political system through a parallel analysis. First, it explores the political content of the new dailies during the four general elections of the period: 1900, 1906, and the two elections in January and December of 1910.[6] The

DOI: 10.4324/9781003254263-1

ways in which all three newspapers represented British election time politics marked a fascinating swinging door moment in histories of British mass democracy. A hugely successful daily newspaper press was representing political news in ways which made the subject matter engaging, accessible, and relevant to the lives of millions of British citizens. Election processes were presented as both exciting and engaging, whilst also being events at the centre of which was the ordinary British man in the street. This simultaneous dramatisation and democratisation of election news made the new dailies a significant form of mass political communication that engaged larger numbers of potential voters than any prior newspaper press that had come before it.

Second, this book investigates some of the ways in which three political parties of the period – the Conservatives, the Liberals, and Labour – responded to the rise of this hugely popular new political press from the launch of the first new daily – the *Mail* in 1896 – and the outbreak of war in 1914. The new dailies emerged during a period of political history in which British politicians had increasingly sought the votes of members of the electorate who resonated with the *Express's* 'man in the street'. Both the new dailies and the three political parties were seeking to simultaneously communicate with the same mass audiences, and therefore the ways in which politicians across the Long Edwardian establishment responded to this new press represents a fascinating insight into a variety of aspects pre-Great War British politics. The differences between each of the three political parties in their reactions spoke of the differing extents to which these new mass-selling newspapers were valued as a form of political communication. These differences between and within the three parties spoke considerably of broader attitudes within Long Edwardian Britain regarding what, in the minds of certain politicians, constituted a viable political press; the extent to which popular newspapers were worthy of effort and attention; and the real value of trying to communicate with the man in the street who, as the *Express* astutely noted, had never held such political power.

The intersection between the new dailies and the Long Edwardian political establishment that this book explores did not exist within a vacuum, however. The significance of the man in the street, both in the political content of the new dailies and within the minds of politicians within three British political parties, built considerably on the back of several decades of cultural, political, and economic developments. Understanding this broader historical context, and the ways in which it influenced both the developments of the new dailies and the evolution of the British political system, is therefore vital.

Long Edwardian Culture

Underpinning much of the new dailies' development within wider Long Edwardian culture was the legacy of the 1870 Education Act. While mass illiteracy had been steadily (if unevenly) in decline since at least the early Victorian period,[7] the 1870 Act's establishment of a framework for universal elementary school education in England and Wales still left a significant legacy. Newspapers had been a primary reading material of the British working classes since the mid-nineteenth century.[8] The 1870 Act, therefore, helped to swell the size of the literate, newspaper-buying mass audiences to whom the new dailies would then sell so successfully.

More specifically, the extent of the 1870 Act's benefits helped to create mass audiences of news readers to whom the majority of traditional British newspapers, 'with their long articles, long paragraphs' and more intellectually demanding news content, had traditionally poorly catered.[9] These audiences demanded newspaper content that was as entertaining as it was illuminating, and that drew on aspects of daily life which resonated with their own experiences. These audiences were steadily catered to in the decades before the Long Edwardian period, as the idea of newspapers being 'representative' of the opinions and tastes of readers gathered credence.[10] Various weekly newspapers in the mid-nineteenth century, most notably the Sunday press, all became hugely popular through news content which combined radical politics with prominent reporting of everyday sensation and particularly crime through stories and images.[11] These popular Sunday newspapers, and early popular daily newspapers such as the *Daily Telegraph*, also benefited from the increasing affordability of newspapers. Growing mass literacy occurred alongside the gradual erosion of the 'taxes on knowledge', which created the conditions for publications to price themselves as affordable options to an increasingly literate mass public. These developments earlier in the nineteenth century were significant, but it was during the Late-Victorian period that the mass potential of affordable and sensationalised everyday news content exploded.

The end of the nineteenth century witnessed the rampant success of a strand of the British newspaper press which prioritised the kind of content that saw the contemporary critic Matthew Arnold famously denounce this 'New Journalism' as 'feather-brained',[12] due its perceived negative impact on the quality and value of British culture.[13] His critique, however, did little to stem the success of a media revolution which took inspiration from the early Sunday press and maximised its commercial potential, and served as a template for the new dailies which would come to define the twentieth century.[14] The New Journalism was particularly defined by a selection of both weekly and daily-evening newspapers that reaped huge reward through their focus on 'brighter, more accessible' news content which simultaneously 'revived' past traditions of entertaining content and marked a 'historic shift' in the history of the British press.[15] Among their most successful titles were newly found 'snippet' publications such as *Tit-Bits* (launched in 1881 by George Newnes) and *Answers*, the million-selling weekly founded by the *Daily Mail*'s founder Alfred Harmsworth.[16]

The most significant of these titles, however, was the evening daily *Pall Mall Gazette* under the editorship of W. T. Stead: the individual about whom Arnold was writing. His 1886 four-part investigative piece into child prostitution – 'The Maiden Tribute of Modern Babylon' – marked a landmark moment both for the *Gazette* (*PMG*) and British journalism, in general.[17] Its graphic descriptions of sexual assault, abduction, and police corruption made the most of the news-reading public's appetite for true crime; it salaciously warned readers of the article's content and drew eager crowds to the paper's office in anticipation of the next instalment.[18]

The *PMG* was not alone; the New Journalism as a whole found success through selling crime stories; the genre and its specific interest in the grotesque and the outrageous proved hugely popular with large audiences of Victorian readers.[19] Crime however formed part of a wider array of news content which the new dailies sold so successfully. This content tapped into newly emergent aspects of late-Victorian and Edwardian culture which resonated with the interests and tastes of the mass British public, especially on an emotional level.[20] In particular, the late-Victorian period, especially after the Bank Holiday Act of 1871, saw the gradual blossoming of a commercialised leisure industry which, by the beginning of the Long Edwardian period, specifically catered to upper-working- and lower-middle-class audiences.[21]

Sports such as football and horse racing, for example, grew into mass spectator events which popular newspapers increasingly covered due to their resonance with lower-middle- and working-class audiences.[22] Similarly, the growth of the popular music hall[23] – estimated at its peak to have drawn over one-million attendees a week in London alone – was part of a swelling of popular demand for theatrics, assisted by new technologies and innovations such as light spectacles and sound.[24] The success of these and other late-Victorian pastimes, notably the seaside holiday,[25] represented the growth of working- and lower-middle-class leisure time, as more of British culture identified the potential to successfully cater to people who had both increased free time outside of work and more disposable income.[26]

Moreover, these increasingly affordable aspects of public life and the ability of the new dailies to successfully cover them were increasingly convenient thanks to the broader 'massification' of Britain in the proceeding decades to the Long Edwardian era.[27] Earlier technological breakthroughs such as the rotary printing press and the electric telegraph helped revolutionise the ease and speed at which information could be sent, received, and distributed throughout Britain.[28] Similarly, the rapid development of affordable railway links between towns and cities connected more people to a greater number of these leisure opportunities, and also assisted the newspapers that reported on those opportunities in reaching a greater number of readers in a shorter space of time.[29] Moreover, these events, spectacles, modes of transport, and the newspapers which reported and relied upon them took place within mass urbanisation, which acted as both a creator and a consequence of this growing culture of mass newspapers, entertainment, and travel.[30]

It was into this population of increasingly leisure-rich, increasingly urban, and increasingly literate British citizens that the new dailies so successfully integrated. They were a hugely successful and significant new addition to a wider popular culture that they simultaneously profited from and continued to maintain. Moreover, despite Salisbury's dismissal of 'office boys', this same mass, primarily urban popular culture that existed at the dawn of the Long Edwardian period was also one of the growing interests to the political parties of the period. Like the new dailies, the political establishment helped to promote the societal significance of the British man in the street, whilst simultaneously seeking to benefit from their growing importance.

Long Edwardian Politics

Underpinning much of the growing political power of the British man in the street were the series of electoral Reform Acts between 1883 and 1885. Building on the earlier reforms of 1832 and 1867, the late-Victorian amendments to constituency boundaries, electoral expense, and voting qualification had a profound impact on the size and composition of the British electorate.[31] The Acts of the 1880s were not without their limitations, as aspects of the reforms' practicalities mirrored past reforms by continuing to limit access to full democratic representation based on geography and gender.[32] However, the consequence of those reforms was an undeniable expansion of voting rights to greater numbers of citizens than any prior period in British history. The total number of eligible voters nearly doubled to almost five million people, and the majority of these new additions were poorer citizens.[33]

More than being just an expansion of the franchise, the political reforms of the mid-1880s furthered the transition of British politics into one dominated by urban centres, as the same towns and cities where the new dailies would sell so successfully during the Long Edwardian period also became the regions where the majority of voters resided, and where the most significant election campaigning took place.[34] Moreover, this transition to a democracy increasingly defined by urban voters was reflected within the behaviour of late-Victorian and Edwardian political parties, as political campaigns on both national and local levels increasingly articulated electoral positions which primarily sought mass, urban, lower-middle- and working-class support.[35] Indeed, the Long Edwardian period witnessed the rise of a new political party – the Labour Representation Committee[36] – which specifically sought to represent the interests of British workers in Parliament.

Furthermore, the wider mass culture of Long Edwardian Britain, including newspapers, also played a significant part of the Late-Victorian shift towards political parties seeking to communicate with the never-more-important man in the street. Historically, newspapers had always been a vital part of political communication in Britain, as politicians saw the communicative potential of publications which educated potential voters.[37] Indeed, politicians throughout the Victorian period directly patronised or part-owned print publications, in significant part to make sure that beneficial messages either about themselves of their party were reaching large numbers of people.[38] This would continue into the Long Edwardian era. A significant portion of politicians who sat in the 1906 Parliament also owned newspapers, and newspapers contributed significantly to successful local and national election campaigns throughout the late-nineteenth and early-twentieth centuries.[39] Other scholarship has also noted the particular political appeal of the new dailies to political campaigners, particularly due to their mass readerships.[40] Newspapers, however, were just one part of an Edwardian evolution in political communication. This is because of recent scholarship which has shown how the same mass culture which the new dailies integrated with, especially spectacle and light innovations, was in turn used by political campaigners, who saw their communicative potential with voters.[41]

The Long Edwardian period, therefore, marked a vital crossroads period between the British press, British politics, and the British lower-middle-class public. First, after decades of gradual evolutions in technology, ideology, form, and purpose, a new mass daily press launched that by the outbreak of World War I was selling millions of copies every single day.[42] This press sold particularly well to a mass audience of urban, lower-middle-class readers whose interests, needs, and pastimes were increasingly better catered by the wider culture surrounding them. Their content successfully resonated with their mass readerships' emotions and aspects of their day-to-day lives, such as sport and consumer pleasures, and helped propel into becoming the most successfully and widely read newspaper press in British history up to that point.

Their success at communicating with their millions of primarily lower-middle- and upper-working-class readers occurred during the same period when the British political establishment was equally enthusiastic about speaking to and with the archetypal man in the street. The consequence of gradual expansions and geographic redistributions to the franchise throughout the nineteenth century was that by the beginning of the Long Edwardian period, all three political parties under investigation in this book were increasingly wishing to speak to an increasingly mass electorate. Crucially, the same potential voters that they were so keen to communicate with were the same urban people who were so readily buying and reading the new dailies. Politicians across the Long Edwardian spectrum were even seeking votes through similar pleas to voters' emotions and livelihoods that were propelling the popularity of the *Mail*, *Express*, and the *Mirror*.

What this book will explore, therefore, is a pivotal period in British political and press history. It will examine the ways in which the new dailies, currently overlooked in existing scholarship of Late-Victorian and Edwardian political culture, represented a hugely significant form of mass political communication at a time when the kinds of people who they were regularly selling to had never possessed more political capital. Their election-time content, explored particularly in Chapter 2, represented political news in a variety of ways which, similar to their better-known sensationalist content, connected the political process to the wider mass culture from which many of their readers drew regular enjoyment. Election news became dramatic, entertainment-laden spectacle which, sometimes literally, illuminated the night sky with colour and noise. The summative significance of the three newspapers' content was to represent general elections as events where the man in the street – the archetypal new daily voter so succinctly captured by the *Express* in 1906 – could engage in ways which were enjoyable, accessible, and connected to parts of their daily existence. Chapter 3 explores the ways in which this mass press centred the political activities and experiences of people who fit within the 'man in the street' archetype, and emphasised their power within the election process. This chapter will also tackle with the limitations, particularly in terms of gender, of this 'everyman' representation of mass democracy.

The new dailies' shared ability was to successfully represent election time political news as both accessible and entertaining aspects of the lives of people who, within the same period, were increasingly a dominant part of the national electorate. They therefore represented a powerful potential space which the political parties of the period could have utilised for their own benefits: a new, valuable form of mass-consumed political communication. Chapter 4 explores the extent to which this potentially rich new form of mass communication was understood by the politicians of the period. The materials explored in Chapter 4 focused initially on the centralised archives of each of the Labour, Conservative, and Liberal party, located in Greater Manchester, Oxford, and Bristol, respectively. To supplement these three primary sites, material was also obtained from other relevant physical archives. These included the papers of David Lloyd George, Andrew Bonar Law, Lord Northcliffe, Ralph David Blumenfeld, and Lord Beaverbrook from the Parliamentary Archives at Westminster; material concerning the early Labour party stored at the Bishopsgate Institute in London; newspaper material accessed through the British Library; and the additional Liberal collections at the London School of Economics (LSE).

The Long Edwardian period was defined by elections which, as existing scholarship as explored in detail, particularly articulated party-political positions which sought mass voting support. The interest in communicating with the kinds of people reading the new dailies, therefore, was an unquestionable priority of the three parties that this book investigates. The extent to which each of the three did, and not did, see the political potential of the new dailies will add vital new dimensions to existing historical understanding of pre-Great War political culture in Britain, and the true extent to which politicians and parties were willing to communicate political messages through a press that was, and continues to be, better defined by its sensational, human interest content.

Notes

1 'I am the Man in the Street', *Daily Express* 12 January 1906, p. 4.
2 Andrew Norman Wilson, *The Victorians* (New York: Arrow, 2003), 590.
3 Hereafter, the Long Edwardian period refers to the time period explored in this book, starting in 1896 (the year that the *Daily Mail* first launched) and ending in 1914 with the outbreak of World War I.

4 The majority of readers of the new dailies are broadly identified by this book as lower-middle- and affluent-working-class citizens discussed by Chris Waters in *British Socialists and the Politics of Popular Culture, 1884–1914* (Manchester: Manchester University Press, 1990) who were primarily urban 'skilled artisans' with growing disposable income. See specifically pp. 1–15.

5 Indeed, the *Mirror* only corrected the commercial failure of its initial launch in 1903 by focusing away from being a 'woman's paper' and aligning more with the man-in-the-street focus of the *Express* and the *Mail*.

6 Those specific time periods being: 26 September to 24 October 1900; 12 January to 8 February 1906; 15 January to 10 February 1910; and 3–19 December 1910.

7 Richard D. (Richard Daniel) Altick, *The English Common Reader : A Social History of the Mass Reading Public, 1800–1900* (Columbus: Ohio State University Press, 1998), 11–12; Alan J. Lee, *The Origins of the Popular Press in England, 1855–1914* (London: Croom Helm, 1976), 33; Michael Sanderson, 'Literacy and Social Mobility in the Industrial Revolution in England', *Past and Present* 56, no. 1 (1972): 75–103, https://doi.org/10.1093/past/56.1.75; Lawrence Stone, 'Literacy and Education in England 1640– 1900', *Past and Present* 42, no. 1 (1969): 118–20, https://doi.org/10.1093/past/42.1.69; Robert K. Webb, 'Working Class Readers in Early Victorian England', *The English Historical Review* LXV, no. CCLVI (1 July 1950): 333–51, https://doi.org/10.1093/ehr/LXV.CCLVI.333.

8 Lee, *Origins*, p. 28.

9 R. C. K. (Robert Charles Kirkwood) Ensor, *England, 1870–1914* (Oxford: Clarendon Press, 1936), 311.

10 Mark Hampton, '"Understanding Media": Theories of the Press in Britain, 1850–1914', *Media, Culture & Society* 23, no. 2 (30 March 2001): 214, https://doi.org/10.1177/016344301023002004.

11 Rob Breton, 'Crime Reporting in Chartist Newspapers', *Media History* 19, no. 3 (August 2013): 245–46, https://doi.org/10.1080/13688804.2013.8201 04; Edward Jacobs, 'Edward Lloyd's Sunday Newspapers and the Cultural Politics of Crime News, c. 1840–43', *Victorian Periodicals Review* 50, no. 3 (2017): 620, https://doi.org/10.1353/vpr.2017.0043; Judith Knelman, 'Subtly Sensational: A Study of Early Victorian Crime Reporting', *Journal of Newspaper and Periodical History* 8, no. 1 (1992): 34–41; Lee, *The Origins of the Popular Press in England, 1855–1914*, 71.

12 Matthew Arnold, '"Up to Easter"', *The Nineteenth Century No. CXXIII*, May 1887, 638–39.

13 Kevin Williams, *Read All About It! A History of the British Newspaper* (London: Routledge, 2010), 120.

14 Adrian Bingham and Martin Conboy, *Tabloid Century: The Popular Press in Britain, 1896 to the Present* (Oxford: Peter Lang, 2015), 3–6.

15 Bingham and Conboy, *Tabloid Century: The Popular Press in Britain, 1896 to the Present*, 6; Geoffrey Cranfield, *The Press and Society: From Caxton to Northcliffe* (London: Longman, 1978), 221; Joel H. Wiener, *Papers for the Millions : The New Journalism in Britain, 1850s to 1914* (New York: Greenwood Press, 1988), xii.

16 Bingham and Conboy, *Tabloid Century: The Popular Press in Britain, 1896 to the Present*, 5–6.

17 Kate Campbell, 'W. E. Gladstone, W. T. Stead, Matthew Arnold and a New Journalism: Cultural Politics in the 1880s', *Victorian Periodicals Review* 36, no. 1 (2003): 20–40; Ann Robson, 'The Significance of "The Maiden Tribute of Modern Babylon"', *Victorian Periodicals Newsletter* 11, no. 2 (1978): 50–57, https://doi.org/10.2307/20085183.

18 Deborah Gorham, 'The "Maiden Tribute of Modern Babylon" Re-Examined: Child Prostitution and the Idea of Childhood in Late-Victorian England', *Victorian Studies* 21, no. 3 (1978): 353–54, https://doi.org/10.2307/3827386; James Mussell, '"Characters of Blood and Flame": Stead and the Tabloid Campaign', in *W. T. Stead: Newspaper Revolutionary*, ed. Laurel Brake et al. (London: British Library, 2012), 25; Greta Wendelin, 'A Rhetoric of Pornography: Private Style and Public Policy in "The Maiden Tribute of Modern Babylon"', *Rhetoric Society Quarterly* 42, no. 4 (July 2012): 375–76, https://doi.org/10.1080/02773945.2012.704120.

19 Richard D. (Richard Daniel) Altick, *Victorian Studies in Scarlet: Murders and Manners in the Age of Victoria* (New York: W. W. Norton & Company, 1970), 9; Megha Anwer, 'Murder in Black and White: Victorian Crime Scenes and the Ripper Photographs', *Victorian Studies* 56, no. 3 (2014): 438–39, https://doi.org/10.2979/victorianstudies.56.3.433; Christopher A. Casey, 'Common Misperceptions: The Press and Victorian Views of Crime', *Journal of Interdisciplinary History* 41, no. 3 (December 2010): 368, 376, https://doi.org/10.1162/JINH_a_00106; Lewis (L.) Perry Curtis, *Jack the Ripper and the London Press* (New Haven, CT: Yale University Press, 2001), 83–108; Judith Knelman, *Twisting in the Wind: The Murderess and the English Press* (Toronto: University of Toronto Press, 1998), 20–44, https://doi.org/10.3138/9781442682818.

20 Shu-chuan Yan, 'Emotions, Sensations, and Victorian Working-Class Readers', *The Journal of Popular Culture* 50, no. 2 (April 2017): 318, https://doi.org/10.1111/jpcu.12535.

21 Andrew Horrall, *Popular Culture in London c. 1890–1918 : The Transformation of Entertainment* (Manchester: Manchester University Press, 2001), 1–6; Chris Waters, *British Socialists and the Politics of Popular Culture, 1884–1914* (Manchester: Manchester University Press, 1990), 20.

22 Raymond Boyle and Richard Haynes, *Power Play : Sport, the Media and Popular Culture* (Edinburgh: Edinburgh University Press, 2009), 19–42; Lucy. Brown, *Victorian News and Newspapers* (Oxford: Clarendon Press, 1985), 271–72; Richard Holt, *Sport and the British : A Modern History* (Oxford: Oxford University Press, 1990), 306–7; Tony. Mason, *Association Football and English Society, 1863–1915* (Brighton: Harvester Press, 1980), 175–206.

23 See Rohan McWilliam, *London's West End: Creating the Pleasure District, 1800–1914*, *London's West End* (Oxford: Oxford University Press, 2020), chap. 11.

24 Richard D. (Richard Daniel) Altick, *The Shows of London* (Cambridge, MA: Harvard University Press, 1978), 509; Ray Johnson, 'Tricks, Traps, and Transformations', *Early Popular Visual Culture* 5, no. 2 (2007): 151–65, https://doi.org/10.1080/17460650701433673; Bernard Lightman, 'Victorian Science and Popular Visual Culture', *Early Popular Visual Culture* 10, no. 1 (2012): 1–5, https://doi.org/10.1080/17460654.2012.637389; Chris

Otter, *The Victorian Eye : A Political History of Light and Vision in Britain, 1800–1910* (Chicago, IL: University of Chicago Press, 2008), 92.
25 John K. Walton, *The British Seaside : Holidays and Resorts in the Twentieth Century* (Manchester: Manchester University Press, 2000), 27–52.
26 The significance of the 1847 Ten Hour's Act in the growth of mass leisure is highlighted by Ross McKibbin, 'Why Was There No Marxism in Great Britain?', *English Historical Review* 49 (1984): 307.
27 Martin Conboy, *The Press and Popular Culture* (London: SAGE, 2002), 95.
28 Joel H. Wiener, *The Americanization of the British Press, 1830s-1914 : Speed in the Age of Transatlantic Journalism* (Basingstoke: Palgrave Macmillan, 2011), 56, 65; Williams, *Read All About It! A History of the British Newspaper*, xii.
29 Mark Casson, *The World's First Railway System : Enterprise, Competition, and Regulation on the Railway Network in Victorian Britain* (Oxford: Oxford University Press, 2009), 36; Conboy, *The Press and Popular Culture*, 107; Lee, *The Origins of the Popular Press in England, 1855–1914*, 21.
30 Michael J. Freeman, *Railways and the Victorian Imagination* (New Haven, CT: Yale University Press, 1999), 121–48; David Paul Nord, 'The Victorian City and the Urban Newspaper', in *Making News: The Political Economy of Journalism in Britain and America from the Glorious Revolution to the Internet*, ed. Richard R. John and Jonathan Silberstein-Loeb (Oxford: Oxford University Press, 2015), 73–106.
31 Luke Blaxill, 'Joseph Chamberlain and the Third Reform Act: A Reassessment of the "Unauthorized Programme" of 1885', *Journal of British Studies* 54, no. 1 (16 January 2015): 88–89, https://doi.org/10.1017/jbr.2014.251; Luke Blaxill, 'Electioneering, the Third Reform Act, and Political Change in the 1880s*', *Parliamentary History* 30, no. 3 (October 2011): 366–67, https://doi.org/10.1111/j.1750-0206.2011.00274.x; Colin Matthew, 'Rhetoric and Politics in Great Britain 1860–1950', in *Politics and Social Change in Modern Britain*, ed. Philip John Waller (Brighton: Harvester Press, 1987), 36; Kathryn Rix, '"The Elimination of Corrupt Practices in British Elections"? Reassessing the Impact of the 1883 Corrupt Practices Act', *The English Historical Review* CXXIII, no. 500 (1 February 2008): 65–97, https://doi.org/10.1093/EHR/CEN005; Richard. Shannon, *The Age of Salisbury, 1881–1902 : Unionism and Empire* (London: Longman, 1996), 76.
32 Matthew Roberts, 'Resisting "Arithmocracy": Parliament, Community, and the Third Reform Act', *The Journal of British Studies* 50, no. 2 (21 April 2011): 381–409, https://doi.org/10.1086/658188; Matthew Roberts, *Political Movements in Urban England, 1832–1914* (Basingstoke: Palgrave Macmillan, 2009), 16.
33 Robert. Blackburn, *The Electoral System in Britain* (Basingstoke: Macmillan, 1995), 74–75; Neil Johnston, *The History of the Parliamentary Franchise* (London: House of Commons Library, 2013), 35–36; Donald Read, *The Age of Urban Democracy : England 1868–1914*, 2nd ed. (London: Routledge, 1994), 441–47.
34 Marc Brodie, 'Voting in the Victorian and Edwardian East End of London', *Parliamentary History* 23, no. 2 (17 March 2004): 225–48, https://doi.org/10.1111/j.1750-0206.2004.tb00728.x; John Davis, 'The Enfranchisement of the Urban Poor in Late-Victorian Britain', in *Politics and*

Culture in Victorian Britain, ed. Peter Ghosh, Lawrence Goldman, and Colin Matthew (Oxford: Oxford University Press, 2006), 95–117, https://doi.org/10.1093/acprof:oso/9780199253456.003.0007; Derek Fraser, *Urban Politics in Victorian England: The Structure of Politics in Victorian Cities* (Leicester: Leicester University Press, 1976), 284–85; Terence Andrew Jenkins, 'Political Life in Late Victorian Britain: The Conservatives in Thornbury', *Parliamentary History* 23, no. 2 (17 March 2004): 198, https://doi.org/10.1111/j.1750-0206.2004.tb00727.x.

35 Jon Lawrence, *Electing Our Masters: The Hustings in British Politics from Hogarth to Blair* (Oxford: Oxford University Press, 2009), 70; Jon Lawrence, *Speaking for the People: Party, Language and Popular Politics in England, 1867–1914* (Cambridge: Cambridge University Press, 1998), 99–127; Susan Stoddart, 'Pressing or Reform: The New Liberalism and Emotion in Edwardian Liberal Newspapers' (Doctoral Thesis: Royal Holloway, University of London, 2014), 113; James Thompson, *British Political Culture and the Idea of 'Public Opinion', 1867–1914* (Cambridge: Cambridge University Press, 2013), 245; Alex Windscheffel, *Popular Conservatism in Imperial London, 1868–1906* (London: Royal Historical Society, 2007), chaps 2, 3, 7.

36 Though originally founded as the LRC in 1900, hereafter the party shall be referred to as 'Labour' for sake (its name from 1906 onwards) for clarity and consistency across the period as a whole.

37 Mark Hampton, 'Liberalism, the Press, and the Construction of the Public Sphere: Theories of the Press in Britain, 1830–1914', *Victorian Periodicals Review* 37, no. 1 (2004): 75.

38 Aled Jones, *Powers of the Press: Newspapers, Power and the Public in Nineteenth-Century England* (Aldershot: Scolar Press, 1996), 175–77; Stephen E. Koss, *The Rise and Fall of the Political Press in Britain* (London: Hamish Hamilton, 1984), 216, Vol. I; Thompson, *British Political Culture and the Idea of 'Public Opinion', 1867–1914*, 63.

39 John Alun Thomas, *The House of Commons 1906–1911* (Cardiff: University of Wales Press, 1958), 14; James Thompson, '"Pictorial Lies"? - Posters and Politics in Britain c.1880–1914', *Past and Present* 197, no. 1 (2007): 202–3, https://doi.org/10.1093/pastj/gtm051; Windscheffel, *Popular Conservatism in Imperial London, 1868–1906*, 54–83.

40 Koss, *The Rise and Fall of the Political Press in Britain*, Vol II: 15–53; David Vessey, 'Words as Well as Deeds: The Popular Press and Suffragette Hunger Strikes in Edwardian Britain', *Twentieth Century British History* 32, no. 1 (7 August 2021): 68–92, https://doi.org/10.1093/tcbh/hwaa031.

41 James Thompson, '"The Lights of the Electric Octopus Have Been Switched Off": Visual and Political Culture in Edwardian London', *Twentieth Century British History* 29, no. 1 (2018): 331–56.

42 By 1910, conservative estimates have the *Mail's* circulation as 900,000, the *Mirror* as 630,000, and the *Express* as 400,000. These numbers exclude the multiple readers per copy extremely likely for each copy sold. See David Butler and Gareth Butler, *British Political Facts* (London: Palgrave Macmillan, 2011), 573.

2 Fighting, Fireworks, and Finish Lines

Election Politics and Spectacle[1]

On Wednesday 26 September 1900, page five of that day's *Daily Mail* featured two columns of news situated side by side that used very similar language. Both stories were headlined using the word 'fighting'. Both stories spoke of 'contests' between rival factions fighting for an overall 'victory'. Key individual figures involved in both stories were presented as directly commanding, or being at the head of, great forces; thousands were moving with them or travelling considerable distance to offer their support to them. These groups engaged in 'heavy fighting' that was represented as being as much about entertainment as violent gravity. Their engagements were described as 'lively', which lent them a sense of excitement; their decisions to 'make a stand' lent a sense of drama to the news, similar to how popular fiction would describe heroic actors in conflict. Moreover, both columns also represented their stories with elements of narrative progression. There were initial sentences that evocatively set their respective scenes: rumours of fighting north of a river; specially timetabled trains running more and more people to a scene that was reaching 'fever-heat'.

Both columns made their news enticing, exciting, and driven by language of violence and confrontation. Their grand arenas of conflict, with their vocal leaders and passionate supporters, were represented to the readers of that day's *Mail* as notably similar in terms of their language used to depict its events, its protagonists, and its overall atmosphere. The two columns however were covering two different kinds of news. The column on the right side of the page was dedicated to stories coming out of the Transvaal,[2] as British troops continued the 'khaki' war against largely guerrilla battalions of Boer soldiers. The column on the left side of the page, with its equally war-like and dramatised, language, was reporting on the first day of the 1900 general election.[3]

DOI: 10.4324/9781003254263-2

This similarity between election coverage and war coverage was not an isolated occurrence, particularly during 1900. The front page of that same day's *Daily Express,* for instance, represented news from elections and from the Boer War in equally similar ways. A column which reported on speeches by Joseph Chamberlain and William Harcourt said that each leader was 'Hit Hard' by criticisms from the crowd, and was indicative of the 'growing fierceness' of the election campaign, in general.[4] Parallel to this article, on the opposite side of the page, there was a headline which spoke of an 'Engagement on the Frontier' where, just as the political fight was reported to be intensifying, the Boers were gathering their strength to 'Wait' the oncoming British advance.[5] The opening day was not exceptional; it was reflective of other coverage across the entire election where political news and war news were worded and represented through headlines in very similar ways. The following week – the first full week of the election – saw both the *Express* and the *Mail* again represent election news as akin to war news. On the one hand, the *Express* portrayed political actions similarly to military manoeuvres, with a report on Liberal MP John Burns's 'hard fight' to hold onto his Battersea constituency which described his retort to a rival speaker as the beginning of his 'counter-attack'.[6] On the other hand, the same day's *Mail* featured news from both theatres of conflict which were headlined and sub-headed in almost-interchangeable ways;

'*AT THE POLLS... The First Fights for Membership... Serious Election Fights'*[7]
   '*BRITISH SUCCESSES... Rundles Force Clearing the Orange Colony... Further Captures'.*[8]

The closeness between representations of election politics and the Boer War continued throughout the entirety of the campaign. In the *Express,* for example, all twenty-three editions published throughout the campaign featured front-page news items that discussed both the election and the war. Furthermore, using a similar initial keyword search of the digital archive, the *Mail* featured fifty-seven individual items which featured both the words 'war' and 'election' within either their headlines or their body content (Table 1). Both papers, moreover, reported on the election using articles that made reference to the contests as 'fights' or involving 'fighting'. The *Mail* featured 104 articles which did this; the *Express* featured the combination of 'election' and 'fight' or 'fighting' 102 times (Table 2). These similarities in language between the coverage of war and coverage of the election of 1900 were far, therefore, from exceptions.

The particular prominence of war-like electoral coverage in both the *Mail* and the *Express* was driven by the centrality of the Boer War both to the political and press cultures of the period. First, the imperial war in the Transvaal was the dominant political issue of the 1900 election.[9] Even as the election was still underway, the Conservatives' large parliamentary majority was credited primarily to their open support for the war, and helped create a legacy for 1900 as a 'khaki' election where popular support for the war was whipped up into a pro-Unionist frenzy.[10] Their pro-war position was strengthened by the electoral position of the Liberals, who were successfully attacked by the Conservatives as 'pro-Boers' and 'Little Englanders' lacking in national and imperial loyalty.[11] The new dailies' emphasis on military metaphors in their election coverage, therefore, reflected, in part, the prominence of the conflict in the addresses and campaign material of both major parties.

Second, the public appetite for news from the Boer War had a profound impact on the British press. For example, the manner in which the *Daily Mail* covered the war was a decisive factor behind its growth in circulation at the turn of the twentieth century. The overtly patriotic nature of its coverage, informed by excellently placed reporters filing news regularly from the front lines, was a huge success, with its readerships more than doubling from the outbreak of the war to its height of over one million daily copies into 1900. The *Mail* was also far from the exception; the majority of British newspapers pursued pro-war editorial stances across much of the Long Edwardian period and helped to create and reflect a broader public appetite for supportive coverage of British military action.[12] Moreover, those few papers which did oppose the war – such as the Liberal-backing *Daily News*[13] – suffered sharp declines in circulation at the same time as the *Mail* was becoming the first daily to sell over one million copies. It is perhaps unsurprising therefore that the new dailies articulated news from the election with particular reference to the ongoing war against the Boers. They were newspapers that were keenly aware and able to articulate content that resonated with large numbers of British people. The similarities between their election coverage and their war coverage were therefore reflective of this broader ability to make their content resonate with popular reader interests.

Interestingly, however, comparisons between election campaigns and military campaigns in the new dailies were not restricted to 1900, which was an election explicitly fought on military policy. Perhaps unsurprisingly however, the coverage during 1900 featured the highest concentration of direct connections between elections and war and conflict, in comparison to the other elections of the Long Edwardian period. For example, direct inferences of elections as 'war' noticeably declined between the election of 1900 and the later elections of the period both in the *Express* and the *Mail,* with the highest number of occurrences post-1900 less than half of that noted during the election coverage parallel to the Boer War (Table 1).

Even with this numerical disparity across the period, each of the other three general elections during the Long Edwardian period were still represented in the new dailies in ways reminiscent of war correspondence. While considerably less frequently, articles which represented election news with reference to 'war', or with reference to a 'fight' or 'fighting', still appeared across all three new dailies throughout 1906 and 1910 (Table 2). The first days of the 1906 campaign, for example, were featured in the *Daily Mirror* as battlegrounds. A page-four report on a constituency contest in Portsmouth was headlined as a 'Novel Election Fight' underneath a broader heading of the 'Present Electoral Battle'. The double emphasis of election contests – whether local or national – as battles was compounded by the article's opening content, which gave prominence to members of the local public being on alert for a potential 'threat';

> *Everybody in Portsmouth is watching the grey motor car...it flits through the town like a battleship.*[14]

The representation of a vehicle carrying around a candidate on the election's opening day as a military vessel was not an isolated news item. The *Mirror* represented election news from various local constituencies throughout the 1906 campaign in ways similar to coverage of war. For example, debates between rival candidates in Manchester on 13 January were described as 'Two Crucial Duels to be Fought To-day'. Along with personal 'duels', where election confrontations were compared to dramatic pistol shoot-outs, regions in the middle of hustings were referred to as scenes of 'The Great Fight',[15] or locations where 'the Electoral Battle Rages'.[16] These metaphorical battlegrounds were also the scenes of election casualties. The 'Great Fight' on 17 January 1906, for example, was reported by the *Mirror* to have claimed the life of Alfred Lyttelton, the former Colonial Secretary 'Killed by Chinese Labour Cry'.[17] The loss of his seat in Parliament, motivated significantly by his role in implementing the 'Chinese slavery' labour policy in South Africa which the Liberals would continually attack in their ultimately landslide victory, was not just a defeat: it was a casualty of a war.

The elections of 1910 would be similarly reported, further reinforcing the representation of elections as battlefields. The *Mirror* again represented general elections in clear military-like terms, reporting on the first day's campaigning in December 1910 both as the beginning of 'the battle of the polls'[18] and 'The Great Fight for Votes'[19] in their opening day's election content. The *Mail* reported similarly as it commenced its coverage of the first of the two elections that year with the dramatic declaration 'we enter the struggle': a line that conjured the image of the pending election as a battle charge from a trench, or a call to stand strong against the violent tide.[20] Battlefield metaphors again featured within a new daily's election coverage. News of Unionist political successes were represented the party having 'gained ground', akin to a battalion fighting for territory.[21] These same victors had 'seen victories in every direction', even after receiving some 'heavy blows' in their efforts to win election.[22] Meanwhile, news from the December election of other, less-successful political candidates were overtly militaristic in their depictions in the *Mail*. Headlines declared news of 'More Deserters from the Party' as Liberal politicians lost their seats.[23] Others meanwhile were reported as being subjected to 'close and stubborn fighting (who) gave and received hard blows'.[24]

Alongside these further representations of battleground elections, with candidates duelling each other and engaging in metaphorical combat to win victory on the field, there were representations of election casualties. In contrast to the 1906 election, where a politician was metaphorically killed, the *Express* in January 1910 reported on actual fatalities that resulted from the election 'battlefields'. Two individuals were reported killed in the process of travelling to vote, with one 'retired colliery official (found dead) at Newsham polling station' and another 'Mr Ernest Turner (who) fell dead... on his way to the poll'.[25] The two others whom the *Express* represented as election fatalities were even more dramatically detailed. One of the pair, 'Mr W. M. Coxten Keen, an artist... was stated at a Hampstead inquest on Saturday to have died from the effect of shouting at an election meeting'.[26] The other casualty (a Mr. 'Percy Boosey') had 'entered into a political argument which ended in blows'; the other participant in this argument – William James England – faced a charge of manslaughter for his involvement.[27] Very much like a real battlefield, election politics was an arena in which human life was reported to be lost.

Across all four elections of the Long Edwardian period, the new dailies consistently referred to elections through metaphorical depictions of war. The election of 1900 was a noticeable high-point of this kind of coverage, with more than double the amount of news items that referred to elections and 'war' than any subsequent Long Edwardian election. However, the continuing references to elections through language of war and fighting still persisted to a significant, if reduced, degree throughout the period. These elections were arenas where combatants fought and were wounded and sometimes died in the effort to win victory at the polls. These persistent representations of election proceedings as violent was not an isolated phenomenon. Rather, it was indicative of broader patterns across the period where news articles which concerned general election politics made hustings, rallies and the process of casting a vote into an exciting and dramatic genre of news content. As well as the metaphorical references to elections as battlefields, coverage across all three newspapers highlighted the drama within the elections. Of particular note was the coverage of election results, which heightened the narrative twists and turns of the overall contests through inventive visual metaphors of election 'races' with rivalling characters battling to the finish line of parliamentary victory. Moreover, these newspapers helped to create the announcement of election results into huge public events, broadcasting constituency results through the use of public demonstrations in parks and music halls. The way that these newspaper-supported live announcements were then covered in the new dailies further represented election politics as a form of mass spectator event; something that demanded, and received, huge amounts of public interest and excitement.

As the next section of this chapter will discuss, this 'sensationalising' of election news, which used linguistic and stylistic innovations similar to the new dailies' better-remembered 'human interest' content, made election politics, and by extension politics in general, into a news genre that was intended to incite greater interest and excitement from the new dailies' readerships. This content made politics engaging, accessible, and entertaining for people historically excluded from the traditional approaches which the British newspaper industry took towards the reporting of political news. Election politics, similar to a football match or a night at the theatre, was a spectacle to which the new dailies' large readerships flocked.

Days at the Races[28]

As was discussed in the previous section, the language of violence – hustings as battles, or debates as wars of words – was a significant feature across the election coverage of the new dailies. The result was political coverage heavily defined by drama and action, lending the stories similar qualities to some of the new dailies more obviously 'human-interest' content which defined their popular appeal. Another key feature of these consistent adversarial representations was the creation of opposing characters. Political parties frequently were represented as binary entities – Empire versus 'Pro-Boer' in 1900, Free Trade versus Tariff Reform in 1906 – that clarified the wider election into clear, easily identifiable sides. In 1900, for example, the *Daily Mail* used the terms "Pro Boer" or "Pro Boers" to describe the Liberals on forty-three occasions throughout their election-time news coverage, and the *Express* nineteen times. These binary metaphorical depictions of Long-Edwardian politics manifested across the new dailies' election coverage most notably in the form of visual results barometers. These cartoons complemented the papers' broader coverage and offered the most striking examples of the ways in which political news was given narrative, drama, and a sense of excitement.

The barometers were large-scale illustrations which tracked the daily state of the overall House of Commons. On the surface, these barometers performed a similar task as other, less extravagant daily summaries of election proceedings, such as tally charts. They summarised constituency results into quickly consumable aspects of the papers' wider coverage, so that a reader could quickly decipher an overall view of the election. However, in contrast to a table of numbers, these visual barometers displayed more than ongoing tallies. Rather, these metaphorical visual depictions of political parties and their parliamentary successes used various dramatic embellishments, such as beads of sweat or the smoke from an engine, embellished these progress trackers with wit, humour, and relatable commentary on the fortunes of particular parties. These subtle visual representations of party-political election progress showcased an intelligence to the new dailies' electoral commentary that far belief their 'feather-brained' historical legacy, as well as their successful ability to articulate political news in similar ways to the 'human interest' content for which they were particularly popular.

These visual barometers most commonly represented election politics, either directly or implicitly, as a race to the 'finish line' of electoral victory. The decision to represent elections as races spoke of two distinct ways in which the new dailies' political content emulated elements of the 'human interest' news that would come to define their legacies. On the one hand, the emphasis on elections as races gave the day-to-day news from the polls a narrative; one that could potentially twist and turn with each new constituency return. This serialisation of political news – the creation of drama which encouraged readers to continue to keep up with the story – tapped into longer traditions of popular publications serialising content. Among the most noteworthy examples of this broader press tradition were the serialisation of works by authors such as Charles Dickens and Arthur Conan Doyle. The former's serialised publication of *The Pickwick Papers* was credited as setting a template for the popular potential of dramatised, day-to-day content.[29] The new dailies' decision to draw influence from these traditions of serialised popular fiction spoke of their ability and desire to represent politics as an exciting news genre from which readers should draw interest and intrigue.

On the other hand, the emphasis on elections as a race, as opposed to another hypothetical battle for victory (such as a tug-of-war or a wrestling match), highlighted the awareness of the new dailies as to the popular appeal of racing news to its intended readership. Racing, and horse racing, in particular, was a hugely successful staple of British popular journalism.[30] The mid-to-late-nineteenth century saw increasing numbers of newspapers including racing coverage, as it was increasingly felt that any paper which neglected the races would fail to attract a large readership.[31] The races, whether attending one in person or betting on a winner closer to home, were a significant part of the lower-middle-class popular culture which the new dailies both catered to and drew influence from.[32] Much like the decision to serialise, the decision to create elections into races showcased a new daily newspaper tapping into its successful brand of human-interest journalism when reporting political news.

The first iterations of the new daily visual barometer featured in the *Daily Express* during the 1900 election and focused solely on the two leading parties and used drawings of each party's leader – Henry Campbell-Bannerman and Lord Salisbury, respectively – to represent the whole parties. Each of the leaders and by extension each party were shown to be climbing one of two slippery poles, and would be lined up parallel to each other with the leading party positioned higher on the page than the other.[33] Moreover, they took up a significant part of a whole page of that day's edition and were frequently the only illustrations on the page. Visually, the two greased climbers were the most striking aspects of the page.

Beyond their size, the competing climbers were significant for their simplification and clarification of the election into a battle between just two individuals. On the one hand, the race only featured the Liberals and the Conservatives; neither the LRC or the Irish Nationalists warranted their own pole climber in the 1900 barometers. To the readers of the *Express,* that election was a two-horse race. On one level, this simplification of the election could be criticised as a 'feather-brained' interpretation of elections; its complexities were overly condensed and thus eroded at the broader reality of the election. While these metaphorical climbers did remove the broader nuances of the election by focusing only on a two-person race, its 'feather-brained' content was less certain. First, considering the limited circulation of the new dailies in Ireland throughout this period, the focus on just Liberals and the Conservatives spoke of the largely non-Irish readership of these papers; for most potential voters reading the *Express,* voting Irish Nationalist was simply not an option. Indeed, the LRC was equally restricted in its national appeal in 1900, considering they only stood fifteen candidates across the entire country and returned two MPs by the election's end.[34] While the focus on just two climbers was undoubtedly simplistic, it also reflected the election realities of the majority of the paper's readers, for whom it was a simple contest between two parties both in terms of a local candidate and their potential place in a future government.

Furthermore, the metaphorical representation of a political party as one leading individual could be similarly dismissed as an oversimplification of the election's reality. More specifically, complex political parties with thousands of local activists, grassroots networks, and potential points of electoral appeal were reduced to their leader. Evidence such as this has been used in debates concerning a supposed growth in 'personality politics' during the late-twentieth century, and how its rise is argued to have weakened the veracity and detail of public-political discourse.[35] In this context however, the depictions of the two parties as individuals further helped to dramatise the election for the *Express's* readers by projecting human qualities onto the political parties featured in the cartoons. As opposed to names on a page, the two parties were given emotional and physical characteristics which fleshed them out in similar ways to characters in a comic strip. More than just giving politics a face, these barometers used emotional expressions on the faces of the two characters to metaphorically comment on the state of each party as the results continued to come in.

Most notably, as the election continued and the scale of Conservative victory becoming increasingly apparent, the visual barometers demonstrated the stark difference in seats between the two parties through additional characteristics that were added to each climber that reflected the contrasting success of the two parties. During the first few days of the campaign, the two climbers are initially shown to be equally exerted, and only distinguishable from each other due to their likeness to either Salisbury or Campbell-Bannerman. However, in order to reflect the growing number of Conservative constituency victories over the Liberals, cartoons printed later in the election expressed the contrasting fortunes of the two climbers. First, having initially appeared directly side by side, the two climbers were soon represented in later election editions of the *Express* at opposite ends of the page.[36] This distance between the two characters – the Conservative climber near the top of the page, and the Liberal climber very near the bottom – also changed over time to reflect the growing Conservative majority; their climber rose up each new day's front page, while the Liberal climber would continue to sit close to the bottom of the page.[37]

Moreover, the Liberal climber was depicted as under considerably more strain the further the election continued. He was drawn with sweat on his brow, and the number of beads would increase as the national Liberal performance became less successful by the day.[38] Nearer the end of the election, moreover, the figure was depicted no longer climbing is greased pole, but instead wrapping his legs and arms around it in a manner which expressed clinging on for safety. The futile exhaustion of trying to keep up the successful Conservative climber lead to him stranded low down both his pole and the page of that day's edition.[39] As the results were finalised, one of the final barometer cartoons showed the Liberal climber looking through a telescope up to the Conservative: a simultaneously humorous and perceptive representation of the gulf between the two parties as the final totals of the future Parliament became clearer.[40] All the while, Lord Salisbury's Conservative climber was represented as increasingly at ease in their ascent to eventual victory. In place of the Liberal's exertion, the Conservative character was shown climbing with little visible effort being put in, and dabbing his brow after reaching the summit.[41] Moreover, his character is shown to have prompted the telescopic actions of the Liberal climber by using a telescope of his own to look down at his rival.[42] This connection between two day's cartoons reinforced the personality and humour that was placed on these metaphorical representations of the election race.

As the election progressed, and the overall result became increasingly certain, the cartoons stopped appearing. Previously used to visually represent a close contest, the two climbers lost their drama and importance as the difference between the parties only grew in Commons seats. Having appeared on every front page since they debuted on 2 October 1900, the greased-pole barometers were included for the last time a fortnight later, with Lord Salisbury the climber sat just enough the masthead with 140 more MPs than the desperately clinging Campbell-Bannerman climber positioned lower and to the right.[43] This decline in the use of daily barometers as the 1900 election's overall victory became more certain was reflected in other parts of the *Express*'s coverage, most notably when, with still over a week of the election to go, the paper felt confident enough to declare to readers in its daily 'Table Talk' column that the election 'for all practical purposes, (was) now over'.[44]

These first uses of a visual barometer by one of the new dailies showcased many of the qualities that later versions across all three papers would also boast. On the one hand, the election contest is visually constructed as a physical contest between rival contestants, with individuals used to represent the party as a whole. Placement on the page was used both to show how the race was going and how close (or not) the 'race' to election victory was. Page placement was also supplemented by changes to the illustrated image to convey the difficulty or ease with which a particular party was progressing in the election. Most strikingly however, the visual races would disappear from the newspaper once the election's overall result became clear. The inclusion of visual barometers, while a striking example of the New Journalism's ability to combine factual clarity with dramatic flair, were seemingly dependant on the narrative of the election they covered; once the ending became obvious, the need to tell the story seemingly became less important.

All of these qualities were further showcased by the visual barometers featured in the *Express* and the *Mirror* (a paper that was reporting on its first every general election) during the next general election in 1906. Both newspapers chose very similar ways to visually represent the race to parliamentary victory. Where 1900 conveyed the race as two rival acrobats climbing slippery poles, 1906 was represented as a literal race: both the Express and Mirror chose to illustrate the election as a battle to a racing finish line between the rival competitors. In the case of the latter, the race was one on foot, with the two leading parties represented by their party leaders as runners, both dressed in sporting attire of vests, shorts and running shoes.[45] Similar to the Express in 1900, the race is shown to be swift and one-sided in favour of the election's obvious early winner; in this instance, the Liberal party. The triumphant Campbell-Bannerman is shown to be confidently bounding towards the finishing line of the Houses of Parliament, with A. J. Balfour (Conservative leader since 1901) behind in a distant second place.[46] Again, much as was the case in the Express in 1900, the cartoons were relatively short-lived.[47] The winner, just as had been the case during the previous election, was clear enough in the early days of the campaign to reduce the want or need for a day-by-day dramatisation.

The Express meanwhile represented the 'race' of 1906 using illustrated motor cars. The choice of motor cars as the racers in 1906 reflected the prominent place that cars inhabited in broader Edwardian culture: Ford's first European plant, for example, was set up in Manchester.[48] Indeed, the previous Conservative government had launched a Royal Commission on motoring in 1905, such was the level of public debate regarding these vehicle's presence in urban public life.[49] Though it was initially featured in a similar size to the greased poles of 1900,[50] these car races became more visually prominent than either the paper's own in 1900 or the Mirror in 1906. At the height of its run, race cars formed a page-wide banner under the front-page title.[51] These illustrations also expanded upon the two-party focus of the others; both Labour and the Irish Nationalists became a part of the race. Changed too was the emphasis on the leaders representing their respective parties. In its place, each motor car had a letter or abbreviated word to indicate which party was where in the broader race to the final election result.[52] Again however, likely due to the fact that the Liberals quickly looked likely to establish a large Commons majority, the cartoons did not last the whole way through the election. Having first featured on page one of the edition published on 15 January, the motor car races featured for a fortnight – the same length of time as the barometers used in 1900 – before stopping on 30 January. Similar to the Mirror barometer cartoons, the 1906 election race lost its place in the *Daily Express* once it was clear the race was already won.

Throughout the 1906 election, the visual representations of day-to-day election summaries featured in the new dailies had evolved beyond the early images of two men climbing greased poles. These illustrated summaries of the electoral successes of political parties combined a concise, clear representation of the political fact with stylistic flourishes that spoke of the interest in drama and narrative so at the heart of the British New Journalism. The figures of returned MPs were recreated as races to a finish line, with participants shown to be either struggling or flourishing in tandem with the wider fortunes of the party they represented. They also spoke of the broader nature of the elections they covered, as well as the other political interests contained in the papers alongside the visuals. Moreover, the appearance and then withdrawal of these cartoons during the span of the election spoke of the one-sided nature of the 'races' to Parliament, with both 1900 and 1906 turning out to be landslide victories for one party only a few days into the weeks-long campaigns. Visually, elections were made to be events of drama and excitement, but only for as long as the winner was not obvious to all.

As well as emphasising drama, these barometers also took forms which fed back into the militarised language used to report on much of the day-to-day polling events. For instance, the *Mail's* coverage of the January election in 1910 featured a half-page visual which represented the British Isles as a colour-coded map, similar to a map of a military battlefield with clear sides and patterns of advancement and retreat. The map, blazoned with the title 'The Progress of Tariff Reform' displayed all of the country's parliamentary constituencies and, through use of different party-specific shading, which party controlled which constituency up to that date of publication. The constituencies, their individually numbered majorities and the visualised 'progress' of the different parties on a national scale were contrasted with the results of the previous election in 1906. The emphasised comparison between the past election and the present campaign helped to further emphasise the extent to which the governing Liberals had 'lost ground' to the advancing Conservatives. While not as obvious a 'race' as the barometers featured in 1900 or 1906, the *Mail's* battlefield map still emphasised ideas of competition and a fight to a finish line. In this instance, the battle for control of the map also reinforced the connection between election news and war news, and how the former was as dramatic and consequential as the latter.

Overall, the use of visual summative cartoons by the new dailies marked a significant part of their broader representations of election politics. The emphases on entertainment within these illustrations varied from election to election, ranging from motor races to depictions of election battlefields, similar to the militaristic metaphors found in election language. At the heart of all these illustrated barometers was the idea that elections were events defined by their dramatic significance. Whether jovial, amusing or attempting the profound, these visual trackers represented general elections as stories of great significance to their readers, and condensed the numbers and figures of the campaigns into striking, easy-to-read images that dramatically summarised who was best placed to hold power in Westminster.

Seen from the Skies

Through their shared emphases on violent language and metaphorical barometers depicting elections as races, the new dailies represented political news in ways which emphasised, and at times depended on, drama and narrative. The coverage gave each elections their own storylines, whether in their coverage of speeches from the campaign trails or in the reporting of daily returns from across the country. The daily returns were paid particular attention across all three papers, in terms of both the page placement and space allocated to the visual

'races', greased poles, and battlefield maps. The prominence granted a
particular race when the victor was still to be decided, and the speed
with which they stopped being published once the overall result was
confirmed, further helped to define the new dailies' political coverage
around narratives of winners and losers as much as by the action and
energy of the warlike language.

Interestingly, the excitable emphasis given to election results was not
solely in the form of cartoon races. One of the other most eye-catching
elements of the new dailies' election coverage were features dedicated
to the public announcement of election results. These articles represented the unveiling of constituency results as eagerly consumed forms
of popular entertainment. Results were announced on large, specially
erected screens in large public spaces, where crowds were shown to
gather in excited anticipation. They were incorporated into evening
music-hall productions, becoming highlights of one of Long Edwardian England's most successful forms of popular entertainment. They
also incorporated lavish technological flourishes to make them even
more of a public spectacle: flashlights lit up the sky to announce a
given winner, or pyrotechnics exploded in different colours to denote
a particular party.

Fascinatingly, the new dailies did not just report these spectacular
public demonstrations; they were involved in producing them. They
were often the sponsors of the music-hall acts; they paid for the erec-
tions of the open-air screens; and they set up special cabling services
to alert theatres of results, to ensure speed of delivery to the audiences
awaiting the news. Not only did they represent election news as show-
case spectator events – events as popular and lavish as anything else
to be found in mass, Edwardian consumer culture – but they actively
helped make them happen. Their dual roles as producers and dissemi-
nators of these extravagant and hugely popular events underlined their
broader emphasis on the excitement of election politics. Such was their
dedication to representing elections in as exciting ways as possible,
they were sometimes prepared to underwrite the excitement's cost.

The high-point of election spectacle took place during 1906, when
all three papers vied during in the early days of the election to give results announcements the grandest of public platforms. The *Mail* dedicated much of page seven and page nine of its thirteenth of January
edition to a feature on the 'monster searchlights' that would illuminate
the skies of London with incoming results.[53] These lights, to which a
page-wide illustration was dedicated, would use Morse code to announce names and parties of constituency victors.[54] Readers were
even provided with a breakdown of basic Morse code, so as to avoid

missing the electoral significance of the public lightshows. Alongside the spectacle, the *Mail* ensured that its dramatic coverage of election news could be easily understand by those it encouraged to take interest in it. Furthermore, in another example of the new dailies' comparisons between elections and battlefields, the *Mail* stressed how similar lights to those used for the election spectacles were used to communicate British messages 'during the South African War'.[55] The various aspects of the light shows – their skyline-defining size, their ease of visibility, and their heavy military overtones – that the *Mail* represented to its readers reinforced the election results as grand events that should not, and possibly could not, be missed. Indeed, their public popularity was sometimes made explicit in the *Mail's* own coverage; people were reported to have 'poured out of doors in countless thousands' in order to see the pyrotechnic results.[56]

The size and spectacle of these light shows was reinforced in the same day's *Mirror,* which also of the 'Results by Signal' lightshows that were going to dominate the London skyline during the campaign.[57] It directly echoed the *Mail's* coverage by describing the demonstrations as dependent on 'monster searchlights', thus again emphasising the large (and by implication impressive) equipment being used to project breaking election results across the city.[58] As well as stressing size, the *Mirror* emphasised aspects of the public demonstrations with overtly militaristic elements. In particular, they reported of red and blue 'rockets' that would accompany the lighting codes to denote a Liberal gain in the case of the former, and a Conservative gain in the case of the latter.[59] The choice by the *Mirror* to emphasise the role of explosive pyrotechnics in the announcement of results added further violence and visual spectacle to the election process, and also further situated their readers at the heart of the election's violence and drama; the explosions happened right in front of their eyes. Moreover, the paper's insistence on the meaning of a rocket's colour – similar to the *Mail's* breakdown of Morse code – ensured that the spectacle of election results was represented in as inclusive ways as possible.

Not to be outdone, the *Express* also produced their own public demonstrations of polling results during the first days of the 1906 election. Like the *Mail,* they too had paid for the use of searchlights to light up the London skyline. Theirs was positioned to light up the sky over the Thames between Waterloo Bridge and Blackfriars Bridge.[60] The *Express* also ensured that readers would 'remember' the meaning of their light shows; the news about the light show included a table of which colour searchlights meant gains for each of the Liberals, Conservatives, Labour and Irish Nationalist.[61] In contrast to the other two papers, however, the *Express* went further than the public light shows. As was outlined on their front page on the thirteenth of January 1906, these sky demonstrations were part of a broader network of public announcements where incoming results would be made 'widely known without delay' in a variety of ways.[62] Chief among these methods of election broadcasting were arrangements by the *Express* with a host of music-hall venues and theatres across London – including the Empire theatres in 'Hackney, Holloway, New Cross, Stratford, and Shepard's Bush' – to incorporate breaking news announcements into nightly performances.[63] The show finales at the London Hippodrome, for instance, would feature the 'highly ingenious' use of on-stage motor cars blazoned with the tallied results of the night's returns, so that the thousands leaving the theatre that night would be fully aware of the overall election picture.[64] Another of the associated theatres – the Coliseum – went further and incorporated election news as a nightly performance highlight. They were reported to have cast one of the acting company as a 'messenger boy (who) shall come upon the stage at the Coliseum immediately after any result arrives, stop the performance, and shout out the figures'.[65] For those unable to attend a performance, the *Express* had also taken steps to get the results known as widely as possible; they had negotiated with a selection of hotels and restaurants so that news would announced to both guests, through spoken announcements, and passers-by in the street through the use of window signage displaying the daily tallies.[66]

The importance of these public news demonstrations, whether in the form of light shows or as part of an evening of popular theatre, is how the dailies demonstrably represented, and even actually helped to stage, election news announcements as exciting news that demanded a popular audience. First, the two primary methods of public dissemination – in the theatre or in the night sky – were forms of visual communication that invited the largest possible audiences to attend. They were large-scale productions which deliberately tried to the entice the greatest numbers of people. Second, they were forms of communication that tapped into distinctive and dominant aspects of late-Victorian popular culture. The use of light shows, much like the visual barometers, drew on the prominence of visual entertainment in Britain since the mid-Victorian period,[67] and the decades of gradual inclusion of lighting and visual innovations which were shaping and impacting significant parts of public and domestic life.[68] Of particular interest to this study was its varied uses in popular culture. For example, illuminations, projections, and pyrotechnics were credited as having helped revitalise popular theatre by the mid-nineteenth century through its ability to 'trick' audiences and provide artists with new ways of staging and producing shows.[69] Furthermore, the London spectacles formed part of a long and rich history of performance culture in the capital, where visuals were great crowd-attracters for a wide variety of public shows and demonstrations.[70] Similarly, as was discussed in the literature review, music hall performances, which were the locations of the *Express's* show interruptions and motor car finales, were an ingrained part of the popular 'everyman' culture from which the new dailies collectively contributed to and primarily drew their large readerships. These election shows, therefore, demonstrated the new dailies' emphasis on elections as entertainment through their deliberate connections to parts of Long Edwardian popular entertainment culture.

For all their drama and their links to the dominant popular trends of the period, there was no denying that these public news spectacles were somewhat restrictive. While their coverage across all three new dailies emphasised their excitement, these were events only physically accessible to those living or working in London at the time. There were, however, additional ways in which the new dailies brought drama to their announcements of election results to both readers and the wider public outside of the capital. The staging and accompanying coverage of mass-attended pyrotechnic displays were complemented by efforts by all three of the new dailies which ensured that readers outside of the capital also received, and were reported as having received, election news in exciting and spectacular ways. One part of the new dailies' broader dissemination of election news drama was the running of special election time trains which carried the same news broadcast during the public entertainment shows to towns and cities across the country as swiftly as possible. The *Mail* was particularly involved in the running of these trains; they and the *Weekly Dispatch* (a newspaper that was also owned by Harmsworth) were the newspapers which paid for the trains, which ran from both Manchester and London. They were reported in the *Mail* alongside the news of the public lightshows, with timetables which outlined their arrival times along various routes which covered much of the Midlands, the South-West, the Lake District, and the North-East.[71]

While not on the scale of the London popular spectacles, the running and reporting of the election trains represented the new dailies' efforts to ensure that the excitement that they represented in election news was as widely accessible as possible. These efforts further than the greater accessibility of geography provided by the trains. Rather, the emphases on the trains as 'Special' mirrored the language used to report on the public shows: the specially set-up telephone lines to theatres; the time and expense put into erecting the one-off lighting apparatus. Moreover, you were not excluded should you be unavailable to attend an event or even make the arrival of one of the trains; news was posted prominently so passers by – the literal 'man in the street' – had to opportunity to be a part of the national spectacle. Regardless of how a new daily reader received the election news, it was represented as a spectacle defined by one-off extravagant efforts which were in their different forms reached millions of people across the country and which all three new dailies had helped to create; they were active participants in news that was not only exciting, but 'special' in ways that allowed huge numbers of people feel part of the occasion.

On Every Wall

For the readers of the new dailies, as this chapter has outlined, news from general elections across the Long Edwardian period was represented across much of the three paper's most eye-catching coverage as exciting and dramatic content. From the first days of publication in 1900, elections were reported with warlike language which inflected all areas of coverage – from candidate's speeches to scenes of both metaphorical and literal polling-station casualties – with a sense of drama and significance that represented elections as arenas that could, and should, be of interest to anyone reading. These war-like reports were complemented by visualised barometers of an election's progress. Sometimes, as was particularly the case in 1910, these barometers heightened the drama and militarised excitement inflected within the dailies' broader coverage; showing election as a battlefield map with opposing sides gaining or losing ground. More generally however, the barometers represented election news as races. These daily updated, page-dominating illustrations featured political parties as human characters which, whether climbing a greased pole, racing their car or bounding towards Westminster, expressed personalities and sense of humour. Their individual actions, such as wiping sweat off of their brow or peering at their opponent through a telescope, provided a nuanced and amusing commentary on the election's broader progress. They reinterpreted daily summaries of news into eye-catching and accessible pieces of entertainment that still spoke convincingly of their broader issues affecting the fortunes of the parties at that given time.

Alongside the accessible commentary and emotional relatability which they gave to the data of daily returns, these 'races' gave elections serialised storylines. The creation of these narratives, as well as being an echo other aspects of popular journalism's most successful content, made elections into a running story with possible twists with which readers needed to keep up to date. More than that however, it was news that, for all its dramatic significance and daily excitement, was engaging and easy to understand. It was also news that the new dailies helped to create, particularly in the staging of public demonstrations of election results. These shows, whether in the open-air or in a multitude of theatres, complemented the barometers by truly making election news a running spectacle that, by tapping into existing popular trends, enticed huge crowds, and popular theatre companies to become a part of them. For those who could not attend the shows, the excitement was directly brought to them at the new dailies' expense in the form of window displays and, most notably, daily trains ferrying news to towns and cities across the country. Regardless of where and how you received the news, the emphasis was consistently on the drama and immediacy of election news; it was news which was so 'special' that it deserved and demanded expensive productions and transportation networks to keep readers up to speed.

The significance of all these different elements of the new dailies' approach to Long Edwardian election politics was that it made elections into uniquely must-read news: it was content that demanded particular attention, both as a piece of entertainment and a consequential part of the lives of the people who comprised the majority of the paper's readerships. This latter aspect of the new dailies' dramatisation of election news – the emphasis on inclusivity of political news – was most spectacularly manifested in a feature which the *Daily Mail* published during both the 1906 and 1910 elections. It was a feature that the paper regularly advertised throughout its election coverage, most notably in 1906 when over a week's worth of election-time editions advertised its availability for 'One Shilling at all Booksellers'.[72] It was a publication in 'Great Demand' which promised to represent an accessible, 'at a glance' summary of the overall state of the election 'in such a way... that they (the purchaser or owner) will have a permanent record of comparison between the old and new Parliaments'.[73]

These two nearly identical documents, published and sold throughout the 1906 and 1910 elections, were colour-coded wall charts.[74] Measuring thirty-nine inches by twenty-four inches, these charts were primarily a map of the country broken up by parliamentary constituency, onto which the owner could themselves track the progress of the national state of the election.[75] This was possible thanks to a set of colour-coded cards that were sold with the chart which were coded similarly to the lights of the light shows: blue for Unionist; red for

Liberal; yellow for Labour, and Green for Irish 'Nationalist'. These different-coloured cards were to be placed by the owner of the chart onto whichever constituencies were won by a given party, culminating in a final colour-coded map of the country showing where the four parties had won their seats in parliament. The coloured card squares were also 'gummed at the back so as to be easily attached'. The charts, printed by the same company four years apart, also featured pre-coded maps of the country before the election, so that a user could, as the advert cited above claimed, compare the colours of their ongoing creation with the map of the existing state of affairs. They also detailed which people were currently in government, minister by minister; explained the differences between different kinds of constituency and how those differences were visually expressed in the shape of the constituency boxes,[76] as well as how to properly apply the correctly coloured squares onto the chart.[77]

Similar to the light shows and the daily barometer cartoons, the *Mail's* election charts visualised politics in an accessible and entertaining manner. They provided plentiful detail about the election to which it was dedicated, such as who was in the sitting government and where the major parties each stood in terms of seats in the House of Commons. These data, however, were a part of a brightly coloured illustration which was almost twice the size of the newspaper which had created it. It represented elections as comparative maps – not dissimilar in design from the battlefield maps used in the main paper – which allowed readers, at a glance, to easily see how the ongoing election was affecting the existing composition of the House of Commons. It was the boldest microcosm of the broader ability of the new dailies to represent election news in a variety of visually and linguistically striking ways that emphasised both excitement and an ease of access.

Fascinatingly, moreover, these election charts also featured one of the other defining features of the new dailies' representations of election politics: the active participation of its 'everyman' readers in the political process. In this instance, the wall charts went beyond making political information accessible to read. Instead, it offered opportunities for readers to actively engage in the political news they were consuming. First, there was the fact that the charts included the coloured cards for readers to themselves place on the map to follow along with the news of daily returns. This portrayed the election news as an interactive exercise, as opposed to an act of passively receiving information. By encouraging this regular reader engagement with the daily news, the wall charts did not only increase the accessibility and entertainment of the election news. It also placed the elections as part of the lives of their readers; it made political participation into a fun daily activity which was both simple and to be encouraged.

It was the placement of election politics within the context of their reader's everyday lives by the new dailies that Chapter 3 will further explore. This will be argued to have manifested in two particular ways across all three newspapers. One of these was how coverage highlighted the prominence of everyman citizens within the Long Edwardian election process: at the polls, travelling with co-workers and family to show political support to a candidate, and as the people whom politicians rightly depending on for their chances of victory. This championing of 'man in the street' political engagement came with limitations, both in terms of the kinds of people and behaviour that was represented as part of emancipated political sphere. However, the collective significance of this coverage was that it represented lower-middle-class British citizens across various age groups as vital and active components of the British political system. They were people – representative of much of the three paper's large readerships – that the new dailies' coverage represented as being in possession of real political power.

The other of these forms represented this power – this significant role within the election process – as being an enjoyable and engaging part of day-to-day life. Elections were exceptional periods of political significance, but they did not interrupt normality. Rather, they were shown to form part of the lived experiences of the new dailies' readers; events to engage with in ways similarly to other aspects of the new dailies' popular content. This normalisation of election politics, twinned with the emphasis on the everyman's political significance, helped to create what the next chapter will expand on as 'everyday elections': periods of political engagement defined both their importance and their compatibility with the everyday lives and habits of many of the new dailies' readers. One of the ways in which the new dailies most notably helped make election news 'everyday' was also a part of the *Mail's* election wall charts. As well as making elections into entertainment, they encouraged readers to put their money where their mouths were.

Notes

1 A version of this chapter was previously published as 'Leaps and Light Shows: Visual Politics in the Edwardian Mass Press, 1900–1910', *Parliamentary History* 40, no. 2 (June 2021): 362–77. Thanks to David Hayton, Brenda McWilliams, and Richard Gaunt for their support both during the original journal process and for granting permission for its evolution into this chapter.

2 'Frontier Fighting', *Daily Mail* 26 September 1900, p. 5.
3 'Fighting for the Flag', *Daily Mail* 26 September 1900, p. 5.
4 'Rival Leaders Hit Hard', *Daily Express* 26 September 1900, p. 1.
5 'More Fighting', *Daily Express* 26 September 1900, p. 1.
6 'Burns and Battersea', *Daily Express* 2 October 1900, p. 5.
7 'At the Polls', *Daily Mail* 2 October 1900, p. 5.
8 'British Successes', *Daily Mail* 2 October 1900, p. 5.
9 See Luke Blaxill, *The War of Words: The Language of British Elections, 1880–1914* (Woodbridge: Boydell & Brewer, 2020), 124–70; Luke Blaxill, 'The Language of Imperialism in British Electoral Politics, 1880–1910', *The Journal of Imperial and Commonwealth History* 45, no. 3 (4 May 2017): 420, https://doi.org/10.1080/03086534.2017.1302118; Paul Readman, 'The Conservative Party, Patriotism, and British Politics: The Case of the General Election of 1900', *Journal of British Studies* 40, no. 1 (2001): 109, https://doi.org/10.2307/3070771; Iain Sharpe, 'Empire, Patriotism and the Working-Class Electorate: The 1900 General Election in the Battersea Constituency', *Parliamentary History* 28, no. 3 (1 October 2009): 411, https://doi.org/10.1111/j.1750-0206.2009.00116.x; Windscheffel, *Popular Conservatism in Imperial London, 1868–1906*, chap. 7.
10 John Atkinson (J. A.) Hobson, *The Psychology of Jingoism* (London: Grant Richards 1901), p. 107.
11 Jonathan Schneer, *London 1900: The Imperial Metropolis* (New Haven, CT: Yale University Press, 2001), 229–60.
12 Simon J. Potter, 'Jingoism, Public Opinion, and the New Imperialism', *Media History* 20, no. 1 (2 January 2014): 34–50, https://doi.org/10.1080/13688804.2013.869067; Gavin Wilkinson, '"The Blessings of War": The Depiction of Military Force in Edwardian Newspapers', *Journal of Contemporary History* 33, no. 1 (1998): 97–115.
13 Bingham and Conboy, *Tabloid Century*, p. 28.
14 'A Novel Election Fight', *Daily Mirror* 12 January 1906, p. 4.
15 'The Great Fight at Birmingham Today—What Will Happen?', *Daily Mirror* 17 January 1906, p. 1.
16 'How the Electoral Battle Rages', *Daily Mirror* 13 January 1906, p. 4.
17 'The Great Fight', *Mirror* 17 January 1906.
18 *Daily Mirror* 3 December 1910, p. 3.
19 'The Great Fight for Votes', *Daily Mirror* 3 December 1910, p. 10.
20 'The Election', *Daily Mail* 15 January 1910, p. 6.
21 Still Leading', *Daily Mail* 18 January 1910, p. 6.
22 Ibid.
23 'Liberal Seceders', *Daily Mail* 6 December 1910, p. 8.
24 'The Outlook', *Daily Mail* 6 December 1910, p. 6.
25 'Election Fatalities', *Daily Express* 17 January 1910, p. 5.
26 Ibid.
27 Ibid.
28 Aspects of this chapter subsection were published as Christopher Shoop-Worrall, 'Scouse Sensation', *Media History* 27, no. 2 (2021): 148–61, https://doi.org/10.1080/13688804.2019.1652583. Many thanks to Rachel Matthews and Guy Hodgson for their editorship of this special issue, and to Stephanie Jones for her support and expertise during the submission and pre-publication process.

29 Jonathan H. Grossman, *Charles Dickens's Networks: Public Transport and the Novel* (Oxford: Oxford University Press, 2012), 54; David Lodge, *Consciousness and the Novel: Connected Essays* (Cambridge, MA: Harvard University Press, 2002), 118.
30 Matthew McIntire, 'Odds, Intelligence, and Prophecies: Racing News in the Penny Press, 1855–1914', *Victorian Periodicals Review* 41, no. 4 (2008): 352, https://doi.org/10.1353/vpr.0.0056.
31 Tony Mason, 'Sporting News, 1860–1914', in *The Press in English Society from the Seventeenth to the Nineteenth Centuries*, ed. Michael Harris and Alan Lee (London & Toronto: Associated University Presses, 1986), 174.
32 Wray Vamplew, *Pay Up and Play the Game: Professional Sport in Britain, 1875–1914* (Cambridge: Cambridge University Press, 1988), 50–54.
33 'Climbing the Election Greasy Pole', *Daily Express* 2 October 1900, p. 1.
34 Andrew Thorpe, *A History of the British Labour Party*, 3rd ed. (Basingstoke: Palgrave Macmillan, 2008), 17.
35 Bob Franklin, *Packaging Politics: Political Communications in Britain's Media Democracy* (London: Edward Arnold, 1994), 23.
36 'Surprise from the Polls', *Daily Express* 3 October 1900, p. 1.
37 'Climbing the Election Greasy Pole', *Daily Express* 6 October 1900, p. 1.
38 Ibid.
39 'Climbing the Election Greasy Pole', *Daily Express* 13 October 1900, p. 1.
40 'Polls Nearing a Finish', *Daily Express* 10 October 1900, p. 1.
41 'Climbing the Election Greasy Pole' *Daily Express* 15 October 1900, p. 1.
42 'Polls Slowly Rising', *Daily Express* 9 October 1900, p. 1.
43 Climbing the Election Greasy Pole' *Daily Express* 15 October 1900, p. 1.
44 'Election Table Talk', *Daily Express* 12 October 1900, p. 4.
45 'Sir Henry Campbell-Bannerman easily beats Mr. Balfour in the race of the elections to Westminster', *Daily Mirror* 17 January 1906, p. 3.
46 'Liberal Seats Recaptured', *Daily Mirror* 22 January 1906, p. 3.
47 The cartoons ceased being included from the 23 January 1906.
48 Jon Stevenson, *British Social History 1914–45* (Harmondsworth: Penguin, 1984), 27.
49 William. Plowden, *The Motor Car and Politics in Britain* (Harmondsworth: Penguin, 1973), 58.
50 'Election Race by Motor-Car', *Daily Express* 15 January 1906, p. 1.
51 'More Sweeping Victories for Liberalism and Labour', *Daily Express* 17 January 1906, p. 1.
52 'Many Ex-Ministers Defeated. Liberal Tide Flows on', *Daily Express* 19 January 1906, p. 1.
53 'To-Night's Results', *Daily Mail* 13 January 1906, p. 7.
54 'How the "Daily Mail" Announces Election Results', *Daily Mail* 13 January 1906, p. 9.
55 Ibid.
56 'Street Scenes', *Daily Mail* 18 January 1910, p. 8.
57 'Election Battle Rages', *Daily Mirror* 13 January 1906, p. 4.
58 Ibid.
59 Ibid.
60 'Where to See Election Results', *Daily Express* 15 January 1906, p. 5.
61 Ibid.
62 'How to See the Returns', *Daily Express* 13 January 1906, p. 1.

63 Ibid.
64 'By Motor Car', *Daily Express* 13 January 1906, p. 1.
65 'Novel Plans', *Daily Express* 13 January 1906, p. 1.
66 Ibid.
67 McWilliam, *London's West End: Creating the Pleasure District, 1800–1914*, 10.
68 See Lightman, 'Victorian Science and Popular Visual Culture'; Otter, *The Victorian Eye : A Political History of Light and Vision in Britain, 1800–1910*.
69 Johnson, 'Tricks, Traps, and Transformations'.
70 Altick, *The Shows of London*.
71 '"Daily Mail" Special Trains from London', *Daily Mail* 13 January 1906, p. 7.
72 '"Daily Mail" Election Chart', *Daily Mail* 16 January 1906, p. 1.
73 'The "Daily Mail" Election Chart', *Daily Mail* 15 January 1906, p. 7.
74 The British Library (BL): 8139.e.23, *Parties at the Dissolution, January, 1906. Election Results Chart. Based on the "Simplex" Chart Designed by Lieut.-Col. Sir J. F. G. Ross-of-Bladensburg* (London: George Philip & Son, 1906).
75 *Daily Mail Election Results Chart* (London: G. Philip & Son, 1909).
76 Ibid., 'Our Election Chart: What It Is and How to Use It'.
77 Ibid., 'Key to Colours'.

3 Everyday Elections and the 'Man in the Street'

As well as advertising their price and their significant public demand, the *Daily Mail's* promotion of their 1906 and 1910 election wall charts also featured a public invitation. On 18 January 1906, for example, the *Mail's* back page announced that readers had just two days left to post in their entries for 'A Prize of £50' which would be awarded 'for the best forecast of the results of the General Election'.[1] The prize was similarly advertised in the *Daily Mirror*, which pronounced that there was 'no time to lose' for those wishing to compete for a prize which was only on offer 'for buyers of the "Daily Mail" Election Chart'.[2] This was also not the first time that the *Mail* had run an election-themed competition. On 29 September 1900, for example, the paper featured an advert in the centre of page seven in which readers, via postal ballots, were invited to test their political knowledge for the chance of a potential prize;

> *All coupons* (posted in from readers) *will be carefully locked up until the election is over, when the sender of the figures most closely agreeing with the result will be awarded a complete set of the "Encyclopaedia Britannia" by way of recognition of his or her skill.*[3]

These election prizes, much like the public results shows discussed in Chapter 2, demonstrated the ways in which the new dailies' political content drew influence from both their own 'human interest' content and wider popular trends in Long Edwardian Britain. Reader competitions had been a hugely successful staple of the New Journalism since its inception, both as items of entertainment and as forums for readers to both literally and metaphorically 'interact' with publications.[4] For example, both *Tit-Bits* and *Answers* had run reader competitions in the 1880s for a house and a pound a week for life, respectively, which managed to attract hundreds of thousands of entries.[5] Moreover,

DOI: 10.4324/9781003254263-3

the *Mail* itself offered prizes during the Long Edwardian period. By happenstance, one of their most extravagant competitions was a 10,000-pound reward for the first successfully completed manned London-to-Manchester flight within a 24-hour period was announced in 1906.[6] The reward was eventually claimed by Louis Paulhan in 1910.[7]

Though the prize on offer was less spectacular, the *Daily Mail* still incorporated this long-standing staple of British popular journalism into its election coverage. Moreover, elements of the 1900 competition echoed the dramatised elements seen in their warlike coverage or election barometers. In particular, the emphasis that entries were 'carefully locked up' lent an air of suspense and importance to this draw, as well as a level of due process and sound prize planning notably lacking from some other popular prize draws, where poorly stated rules led to a near-ruin of the successful popular author Edgar Wallace who promoted a competition in the *Mail* in 1906.[8] Most significantly, however, was how the election competitions contributed to a broader pattern of 'everyday election' news coverage, where politics was closely related to the lives and everyday interests of the man in the street who symbolised the majority of the new dailies' readerships.

The collective significance of the everyday election content, this chapter argues, is how it blurred the restrictive historical line between press coverage of the British political sphere and the everyday lives of the British lower-middle classes who comprised much of the new dailies' audiences. First, election news was represented in ways which intersected with elements of day-to-day British life, in particular, through its use in product advertisements.[9] These adverts, which told election news through humorous connections to the products being displayed on the page, directly related politics to elements of everyday life such as food, drink, accessories, and furniture, in ways that made elections into an integrated part of a reader's daily news consumption. This wider distribution, and the links to everyday products and parts of a reader's typical lived experience, represented politics as an everyday part of life: a significant step away from the restricted world represented through historical political newspaper content which largely defined political news as primarily concerning verbatim speeches from Parliament.

Second, the new dailies' representations of 'everyday' political news emphasised the prominent role played by their readers in the election processes of the period. Collectively, the three papers articulated an image of a political everyman: the ordinary member of the public upon whom British politics depended. This everyman ideal had its democratising limits. Certain kinds of people and certain kinds of public behaviour were deliberately excluded, which drew a clear line between what and who was allowed to be seen as part of the politically powerful everyman identity. These limitations were undeniable, but the summative result was still an image of election politics where the British mass public – symbolised by the recurring motif of an 'everyman' – had never had a greater stake in political life. The everyman was very similar to the 'man in the street' whom, as scholarship discussed in Chapter 1 identified, politicians across the Long Edwardian spectrum sought support from on the campaign trail. The everyman was shown to be enjoying their significant place in the political system as they travelled to cast their votes, or showing their support on the streets with work colleagues and family members. This everyman was also a widely applicable identity which encompassed various age-groups, professions or geographical locations. The consequence was a collection of election content which, similarly to the dramatised coverage, made election politics into an exciting and easy-to-access aspect of everyday life. More specifically, however, it created a strong positive connection between electoral engagement and the everyday lives of the new dailies' readers, who were collectively represented through the idealised everyman.

Political Product Placements

On 9 December 1910, page eleven of the *Daily Mirror* featured a page-dominating item which declared 'A Popular Victory' in which the victor in question had won a 'Sweeping Majority' against their inferior competition. This 'Special Election Result' was not however related to election news, but instead to a company which was advertising its 'Ironclad Gas Mantles' where its 'British Made' products had defeated the 'All Other Gas Mantles' which were its competition.[10] The direct connections made by this advertisement to the ongoing election of the time were stark. The language used in this advertisement, most notably the advert's headline pronouncing a 'Special Election Result' was nearly identical to language used in the same newspaper to report on and headline election news. Indeed, particularly through the use of the word 'sweeping', it even conveyed the same sense of the dramatic as the daily news discussed in Chapter 2. Moreover, the advert itself was formatted to look like a ballot paper, with the two options – the advertised product and its competitors – presented similarly to the cards which electors would fill out at a polling station, complete with empty boxes into which a mark could be placed against one of the two choices.[11]

This fireplace advert was not an isolated occurrence. All three new dailies featured advertisements which directly referenced Edwardian election news as part of their efforts to sell products to the three newspapers' readers. These electoral references, which ranged from targeted comments on a given day's big election news to visual formats which evoked campaign posters and ballot papers, spoke considerably the prominence of the elections in the minds of the new dailies' readerships. The fact that certain advertisers deliberately represented their products through electoral references represented how the elections were a likely topic of daily conversation of the millions reading these newspapers every day. Moreover, the often-humorous ways in which the election was used in these attempts to sell a variety of household products further represented election politics in the new dailies as an accessible and enjoyable genre of news content, which helped stimulate the popular appeal of election news which they simultaneously trying to tap into to sell their goods.

For instance, some of these politically themed advertisements referenced election news in general terms which were not specific to either a particular election or an item of news. For example, other companies besides the fireplace advert featured in the *Mirror* referenced some of the print material that featured during elections. An advert for the hot drink Bovril, printed in the *Daily Mail* in early January 1906, gave the reader two choices to vote for: 'BOVRIL or INFLUENZA'.[12] Another company, a clothing company which advertised on page two of the *Mirror* during the January election of 1910, featured a table with a cross of approval next their project, in order to emphasis its supposed victory over the competition.[13] Others, also featured in that January's editions of the *Mirror*, resembled the placards and posters carried by party agents or members of the public which pronounced support for a particular party or politician. Two such-styled adverts featured in the twentieth of January's issue, one which campaigned for a 'Vote for Oxo'[14] and another, also for a meat-based hot drink, which appealed for 'The Candidate for Health'.[15] Like the allusions to polling cards, these placard-like adverts made a direct link between physical aspects of Edwardian election culture and the everyday products they were attempting to sell. The references by these advertisers to physical election practice – whether the casting of a vote or the showing of political support – spoke of the significance they placed on election references as a potential selling tool. In turn, this spoke of the broader everyday popularity of election news which the new dailies had both helped to foster and tapped into through their popularised news content.

The imagined popularity of election news in the lives and minds of the new dailies' readers, which certain advertisers both keenly sensed and helped to maintain, was reflected by other adverts which made generalised references to elections and popular engagement with politics in their attempts to market their products. A consistent theme across these election-themed adverts for a variety of household products was an emphasis on an appeal to the public, as if a particular product was a politician seeking the public's support. Across a single week in late January during the 1906 election, for instance, the *Daily Express* featured adverts which metaphorically represented their products as election candidates who were in the process of obtaining, or that had already obtained, the necessary popular support to 'win'. There was the 'Popular Candidate' who was standing for Cadbury's Cocoa[16]; the question put to the nation was claimed to have led to the people electing Bovril[17]; a government guarantee that Cope's 'Bond of Union' will be the popular choice of cigar.[18] There was also a humorous advert which proclaimed the 'major success' of a different kind of MP: Maypole Tea, the other kind of 'victory in this January poll'.[19] During the same election, similar adverts which featured products as campaigners who were either seeking or basking in popular support appeared in the *Mail* and the *Mirror*. Interestingly, the same companies featured across more than one of the new dailies: Maypole Tea urged readers of the *Mail* to 'Poll Early and Often' in its support of their 'universally popular' product the week before they announced their 'MP' in the *Express*.[20] Another business, the Midland Furnishing Company, advertised in both the *Mail* and the *Express* two days apart using similar items: their products were 'unanimously elected' in the former due to their quality and fair price.[21]

Another furnishing company, based north London, used similar calls for electoral support in simultaneous adverts in both the *Express* and *Mail* published on 17 January 1906. The advert used in both papers called for readers to 'VOTE! VOTE!! VOTE!!!'[22] for their products, which mirrored the other election-time adverts in the way it made a broad link between the product being advertised and general elections. In contrast to the Midland furnishers, whose advert appeared in the *Mail* the following day, the Hackney company made a direct reference to one of the key electoral issues of that election as part of their pitch. First, they promised prices that represented 'Fair Trade, Free Trade, Honest Trade'.[23] The second of their three promises directly echoed one of the Liberal's key electoral pledges during 1906 of economic free trade, which was part of a big-load versus little-loaf electioneering strategy aimed primarily at prospective lower-middle and working-class voters. Second, the final line of the advert stated 'You Want Protection', which similarly echoed one of the leading Conservative policy promises: a reform on import tariffs to preferentially benefit British and imperial suppliers.[24]

The significance of this issue-specific election-themed advertisement was that it was more detailed and nuanced than the more generalised references that were made by other adverts which mentioned candidates or electoral victories. Its use of election-specific details in its product pitch mirrored elements of the election barometers; they added to the new dailies' wider inclusion of nuanced political news and commentary as part of the human-interest election content. The references to specific detail in these clear yet tongue-in-cheek electoral references also lend greater credence to the argument that, far from feather-brained, these light-hearted election items required and encouraged a reader to engage with the serious matter at the heart of the humour.

The Hackney advert was also not an exceptional example. They were one of several companies whose advertisements across the Long Edwardian period featured election references that were specific and knowing of particular pieces of news from the election in which they featured. One of those other businesses, interestingly, was the Midland Furnishing Company; they promised 'Fair Trade and Protection to Customers' to the readers of the *Express* on the previous day to the Hackney advert.[25] Another company, Wright's, advertised their coal tar soap on the same day as the Hackney advert using similar references to the key debate of the election. As well as declaring that their soap 'has held the seat for 40 years' and 'is unopposed in every Nursery Constituency', the advert labelled the product as 'The Protection Candidate': a direct reference to Conservative candidates who were campaigning throughout that election on a tariff reform platform.[26]

The tariff-free trade debate was not the only election-tailored references featured in advertisements across the new dailies in 1906. One advert featured in both the *Mail* and the *Express* humorously framed their product around the issue of Irish Home Rule. It was a cartoon which depicted Campbell-Bannerman and Balfour in rare agreement over 'The Real Home Rule Question': the superior quality and prices of the furniture that they were both inspecting.[27] Another advert featured a crude phonetically written endorsement for a product from a Chinese 'slave': a direct reference to one of the most controversial aspects of the campaign which rivalled free trade as one of the leading Liberal lines of electoral argument.[28]

Adverts during the 1910 elections also made specific references to issues and debates specific to the period, in particular, the constitutional 'Peers versus the People' divide between the Liberals and the

Conservatives. Maypole Tea, for instance, proclaimed that their product was 'The Voice of the People',[29] while a Grimsby-based supply company claimed that their offerings of 'fresh fish, cleaned ready for cooking' were deserving of the attention of both 'Peers and People'.[30] Flor de Dindigul, meanwhile, declared their product as 'The Peer of Cigars at the Common Price': the words 'peer' and 'common' were both underlined, as if to avoid any doubt in a reader's mind as why those particular words may have been used.[31] The constitutional debate was also not the only election issue included in advertisements throughout 1910. Most notably, a Unionist pledge during the December election for a public referendum on tariff reform was referenced by adverts for multiple companies. Dunlop, most notably, underlined the word 'Referendum' in their claim that a public poll of British motorists would 'invariably result' in a favourable opinion on their products.[32] Once again, election politics – and issues specific to that particular election – were represented as a key selling points of a product, which emphasised the success of new daily content in situating political news within the everyday life of the 'man in the street'.

Alongside specific election references, one particular company also utilised running election commentary in their adverts; messages which humorously related their product to daily news from the campaign. The company in question – Bovril – featured adverts throughout the 1906 election which commented on the ongoing troubles of the Conservative party, as they slipped from early election optimism to a swift realisation of parliamentary defeat. Before the scale of the Conservative defeat became apparent, an advert on 16 January used the words of a pre-election speech by Joseph Chamberlain – "give me my chance and let me see what I can do" – alongside an identical pledge from the Bovril candidate.[33] This representation by Bovril of the early Tory optimism was swiftly followed by adverts in both the *Mail* and the *Express* which directly referenced and mocked the decline in Tory fortunes as part of their product's pitch. In the *Express* from 23 January, Bovril offered 'Advice to Unionists! Nevermind! Take Bovril'.[34] The previous day's *Mail* featured a similarly joking 'Message from Birmingham' from Bovril which offered encouragement to Unionist voters disappointed by the results;

Are you down-hearted? Take Bovril...
at any rate, ONE PROTECTION CANDIDATE (Bovril) holds his seat.[35]

As was particularly prominent in Bovril's running commentary of Tory electoral failure, advertisements featured in the new dailies' Long Edwardian election coverage incorporated election details in amusing and knowing ways. These joking references to either winning the people's vote or consoling the losing party represented election politics as more than entertainment. The presence of election items within advertisements situated election politics as an enjoyable part of everyday life through its enjoyable connections to food, drink, and household items. They also emphasised the accessibility of the new dailies' election content; they placed items of election news – contained within the humorous adverts – outside the election articles themselves. Readers who purchased and consumed any of the election-edition new dailies would find election news – presented in similarly easy-to-understand and entertaining ways – across the entirety of the paper next to content usually disconnected from political news. The adverts cited in this chapter appeared both on pages of each of the new dailies without any other election news items, as well as on pages where election news was featured. Elections, therefore, were not a subject matter restricted to certain pages; it was news that could be picked up across virtually any page of a new daily.

An additional significance of the election-themed advertisements was the way that it represented politics as connected to the lives of the women reading their papers, as well as the men. Much of Long Edwardian Britain consumer culture, of which advertisements were a significant part, was directed primarily at a female audience. Methods of engagement with consumer culture, and, in particular, the act of shopping, had been keenly associated with women and femininity since at least the mid-Victorian period.[36] The advertisers who were marketing lower-price domestic products such as Bovril (which featured the most election references in the new dailies), drew particularly on ideas of gendered domesticity in their targeting of women.[37] Therefore, it is important to understand that the new daily readers to whom these everyday election references were being pitched to were not exclusively male.

Moreover, certain adverts which featured election references promoted products exclusively were women. The *Mirror*, for example, which had originally launched as a women's paper before a radical overall due to disappointing sales, featured adverts during both the January and December elections of 1910 which pitched election content squarely at female readers. The former election carried an advert for W. B. Corsets styled as a ballot paper, which proclaimed that there was in-fact 'no election necessary' to determine their product's market superiority.[38] The latter election featured a 'Referendum' for two fragrances – 'Courvoiser's two choicest perfumes'[39] – and a 'vote for Camp Coffee' which featured a female cartoon character on the campaign trail on behalf of the product.[40] While the latter product was not as exclusively tailored to female consumers, its use of a female activist further placed election content within newspaper content which was principally aimed at female readers.

The election adverts explored in this chapter, whether directly or indirectly, articulated political news in ways which did undoubtedly place election politics within the context of certain lived experiences of Edwardian women. However, this was not representative of the papers' broader inclusion of women in their election content. The new dailies' representations of election news, such as was included humorously within adverts for an array of cheap household products, were undoubtedly accessible and positively placed politics within reach of the everyday lives of millions of primarily lower-middle-class Britons. However, this political inclusivity came with some strict limitations. Specifically, there were limitations of gender and forms of acceptable electoral behaviour that placed parameters on who or what was permissible within the papers' shared representations of mass 'everyman' political culture. These limitations also spoke of the predominantly masculine election culture of the period, as was noted in Chapter 2.

Men in the Street

Page four of the *Daily Express*, published on 17 January 1906, featured a feature on the 'Two Types of Successful Lady Politicians' which claimed the election had 'brought no revelation more startling than the influence of women in the great battle of the polls'.[41] Their 'arrival' onto the electoral scene was reported as comparable to the decisive Prussian intervention at the Battle of Waterloo; another example of the new dailies' dramatisation of election news through military references explored in Chapter 4. Despite these declarations however, the influence with which women were credited spoke more of their electoral exclusion in the new dailies than their 'startling' political impact. Their significance was represented as being similar to polling sirens: their 'personal charms' are enough to encourage men to vote. They 'commanded' men and so, as one interviewee was reported to have said, there was no point in women themselves having the vote. The other type of 'lady politician', incidentally, dedicated none of their time to active campaigning. Instead, they accompanied their husbands who were the actual candidates and the party agents, and met with 'small gatherings of wives and mothers'.[42] The *Mirror* meanwhile represented women in one instance as cheerleaders to the election action who showed their political engagement through a similar dedication to appearance and 'charms'. As Balfour continued his re-election campaign around Manchester, for example;

> *several young women waited (*at the door of the meeting space*) with the avowed intention of kissing the ex-Premier, an embarrassing compliment (*which he*) laughingly succeeded in avoiding.*[43]

The same paper's description of women during the same election as 'servant girls'[44] accurately summarised their collective role in the new dailies' representation of elections. Female contributions were depicted, in the very few instances where women were represented as part of any of the four general elections of the period, as minimal and background. The roles of electioneering women were defined by their ability to console, charm, or flatter. The absurdity which the new dailies placed on the idea of women playing an active role in Long Edwardian politics outside of gendered feminine roles of comfort and flirtation was compounded by the *Mirror's* profile, covered on two separate pages, of the 'First Lady Voter'.

The individual in question – 'Miss Alvin Bussey', an operatic teacher – was reported as 'the one women who has voted in the parliamentary election'. This reality came about, the article reported, because of political papers being posted to her address by happenstance. The fact that this event was a mistake was heightened by the article due to references in the article to the shock of those she encountered on her way to vote: the 'embarrassed election officer' unsure of what to do; the policeman who 'laughed' at Miss Bussey when she arrived to cast her vote.[45] An isolated instance where a Long Edwardian woman engaged in election politics, beyond using their 'charms', was represented in the new dailies as a joke, such was its absurdity and lack of place within their 'everyman' interpretation of accessible election politics.

The narrowness of this 'everyman' archetype should be further interrogated. The new dailies, as explored in Chapter 1, were successful due in large part to their tailoring to imagined reader interests. Newspapers like the new dailies, however, deliberately defined their imagined readers differently by their gender, with 'women's sections' particularly emphasising news content connected to feminised domestic roles.[46] Moreover, elections within Long Edwardian Britain have been previously noted as dominantly masculine spaces. Women were also denied the legal right to a national electoral note until 1918, and even then only on limited terms.[47] It is therefore unsurprising, perhaps, that the new dailies would particularly promote an every*man*.

However, the fact that the new dailies had women's sections spoke to the fact that a significant proportion of their readership were imagined to be women. Moreover, as mentioned previously, aspects of massified Long Edwardian Britain, however simplistically or crudely gendered, were primarily catered towards women. Moreover, women did navigate and challenge gendered spaces across mass-entertainment and pleasure industries, from the music hall to association football, both as participants and spectators.[48] Women similarly were active and present within 'masculinised' political spaces such as the House of Commons,[49] and worked during the January election of 1910 collecting petition signatures across hundreds of constituencies as part of an 'unofficial' referendum on women's suffrage.[50]

Moreover, recent scholarship by David Vessey has explored the ways that women within Long Edwardian politics and the sensationalism of the new dailies intersected in complicated ways. Through an analysis of representations of Women's Social and Political Union (WSPU) campaigns, in particular, hunger strikes, some of the complexities of the period's mass 'everyman' culture is untangled. On the one hand, the new dailies were broadly hostile towards campaigns for women's suffrage: the gendered language of 'hysteria' featured prominently in dismissals of efforts for electoral equality. On the other hand, those same new dailies did provide a multifaceted platform within which debate surrounding women's suffrage occurred. Knowledge of the new dailies' particular use of sensationalism – something which was a key element of their broader, everyman-inclusive election coverage – was something suffrage campaigners deliberately utilised, especially regarding the issue of the forcible feeding of activists on hunger strike.[51]

Therefore, the new dailies' near-total exclusion of women from their representations of general elections, within their editorial coverage at least, belied the complexities of gender both within the politics and mass-entertainment cultures of Long Edwardian Britain. The electorate of the period, and much of the culture that fed into new dailies' success, was profoundly gendered in ways that did give an imagined 'everyman' particular cultural and political capital. It is a lie however to articulate – as the new dailies largely did throughout their coverage of these four general elections – that women were absent from, nor passive within, these cultures. There was not, however, a similar level of significance granted to an imagined 'everywoman' by the new dailies and their articulation of mass election politics.

It was not only women who the new dailies represented as outsiders to their interpretation of inclusive mass politics. There were also multiple references to 'rowdyism': violent and disorderly behaviour which was reported as disgraceful and unbecoming components of the election process. There were clear distinctions between the positivity of the entertainment-inflected references to election 'fights' and the negative references to violent voters. For instance, the sensationalism of a *Mirror* article which celebrated a contest as an 'Electoral Battle' also referenced 'hooligans' who were threatening the Conservative candidate.[52] The same day's paper also reported on 'wild scenes' from the East London constituency of Limehouse where 'fierce free fights' had resulted in several people receiving 'serious injuries'.[53] Similarly, 'flour bags and more dangerous missiles' had been 'flung about' in chaotic scenes which had left a successful Liberal candidate 'suffering severely from a heavy blow'.[54]

These critical representations of election violence were noticeably different from the dramatised battlegrounds of election entertainment from Chapter 2, through the emphasis on disorder. The dramatic violence explored in Chapter 2 which injected election news with sensation and everyday interest was frequently described in energetic and kinetic ways, but was never described as 'wild' or with anything involved being 'flung'. Moreover, public contributions to political meetings were not completely dismissed. For example, heckling speakers or the 'battle between the heckler and the candidate…a tussle for the cheers' was reported by the *Mail* in 1900 as a 'joy' and a welcome part of the platform.[55] Mass political participation was therefore represented as permissible, but only to those who could engage in a suitably respectable manner. The dismissals of rowdy electors, and specifically those who engaged in physical intimidation and violence, echoed ideas about extensions to the British franchise since the mid-Victorian period. Within this context, democratic participation was a reward for 'respectable' citizens from lower-middle or upper-working-class backgrounds who conducted themselves in a suitably non-aggressive manner.[56]

This neo-Victorian emphasis on respectability and an aversion to physical violence was an undeniable part of the 'everyman' culture which the new dailies represented. It stood alongside the papers' dismissals and exclusions of female political participation as a significant limitation on the accessibility of the political content. The chaos within the reporting of negative violence set it, and the people who participated in it, apart from the acceptable forms of political engagement which formed part of the new dailies' everyman mass culture. For all the attention to accessible drama, sensation, and humour, there were certain populations of people who were excluded from the political content of all three papers across the whole of the Long Edwardian period. The kind of person whom all three papers did include in their election content was summarised by an article in the *Express,* published on the first day of the 1906 campaign, which claimed to contain the opinions of 'the Man who can Control our Destinies'. This individual, mentioned briefly at the beginning of Chapter 1, was given a clear set of features and opinions that spoke of who, specifically, was at the heart of the new dailies' everyday election content. After each declaration, the voice repeated their identity; 'I am the Man in the Street';

> *(I am) generally not a politician... a teetotaller, anti-vaccinationist, or a vegetarian, or any sort of crank... industrious... casual and intermittent interest in football matches and race meetings... I like the theatre and the music hall – the latter, perhaps the more... sympathetic, but not sentimental... England for the English, a happy England populated by prosperous Englishman.*[57]

This 'man in the street' given voice in the *Express* was the everyman who resonated across all three new dailies' election content. His interest in sport, the music hall, and visual spectacles could be seen in the use of the election barometers and results announcements, as well as the broader references to elections as battlegrounds and action arenas, discussed in Chapter 2. It was his life to which the vast majority of advertisers discussed earlier in this chapter were pitching their election-themed products such as hot drinks, tobacco, and affordable furniture. Moreover, while he may not have been a politician himself, he was at the heart of the process; his letterbox was 'crammed' with election leaflets and candidate after candidate tried to shake his hand in hope of support.[58]

Indeed, all three newspapers made politics an important and entertaining part of his day-to-day life. Articles focused on citizens who were engaging in elections in a variety of ways, ranging from the casting of votes to sharing laughs with those they wished to elect. By doing this, political news was represented to be both fun and flattering for the everyman reader. On the one hand, election politics was shown to be an enjoyable and amusing field of daily life. On the other hand, it was a process where they – millions of urban, lower-middle-class British male citizens – had as much power and influence as the politicians and parties they supported. Moreover, whilst still considering the significant limits on gender and respectability imposed upon the new dailies' idealised political everyman, electoral engagement was represented in ways which included virtually any age of Edwardian everyman.

Schools and Surgeries

On 5 December 1910, there was more than one election being held in Britain. The smaller of these, reported on pages three and ten of that day's *Daily Mirror*, was held at a school in Kent where schoolboys were 'holding a general election of their own'. Besides the more apparent aspects of any election such as 'taking sides, designing posters, election agents, arranging meetings' the article noted that it was illegal for a boy to treat another of the boys with food in order to win his vote.[59] Though the results were never followed up on, the two-page profile of a school election showcased how the enjoyable privilege of election engagement was open to everyman from a very early age. Moreover, the engagement went beyond the surface of making posters; there was the code of ethical behaviour (no treats from the tuck shop in exchange for votes) which mirrored the 'real' elections which were occurring at the same time. The fact that the schoolboys faced the same strict rules of voter engagement as 'real' candidates – an issue which was discussed in the same paper two days before[60] – made the report more than a simple piece of enjoyment. Rather, it showed that it was never too young to learn and engage with the realities of electoral life, provided again that you were a boy.

Likewise, it was never too old for an everyman to engage with the politics reported in the new dailies. The *Mail* reported of a voter who 'if all goes well' would have been aged 102 by the time the election came to an end. This 'veteran' with a 'total family of 182', similar to the school election reported by the *Mirror*, represented the extent to which everyman of all ages could and should participate in elections.[61] Both the children and the centenarian were held up as examples for readers through the positivity given their political enthusiasm. Their identity as extremes at either ends of their life, with schoolboys, on the one hand, and a centurion, on the other, suggested that any everyman in the middle was equally able to engage in the elections. These age-dependant individuals were not isolated figures. Members of the public were represented as active parts of the election whose various methods of engagement were reported to suggest that such behaviour was to be celebrated and emulated.

The most concise occurrence of various kinds of everyday election role models featured in a double-page spread at the centre of the *Mirror* on the seventeenth of January 1910. Featured as part of a summary of campaigning that was occurring across 'sixty-six' constituencies, the paper featured a collage of photographs of voters from across the country who were casting their votes. Three of the five photographs featured various motor vehicles: a motorbike carrying personalised campaign slogans (as well as an elderly passenger) around the town, and two trucks carrying citizens to where they needed to vote. One of these latter two, depicted ferrying a group of voters to their polling station, was a fire engine, where the crew appeared to have volunteered their time to drive around Fulham. Where these three images showed good citizens using their free time to engage themselves and others with the ongoing election, the other two featured individuals who were overcoming significant personal strife in order to vote. The two men in question – the top left and bottom right images – were both in wheelchairs as they travelled to or from the polling station. The former 'invalid' was photographed having cast his vote, being supported by electioneerers, fellow voters and two police officers. The latter, who was pictured being helped into a taxi by two other men, was leaving his hospital bed at St. Thomas's Hospital in order to vote in his Brixton constituency station.[62]

As well as successful voting stories, there was a story published by the *Mail* during October 1900 of an aspiring voter who was only denied by the people at the polling station. The man in question, having been handed a voting paper, was unable or unwilling to cast his vote by the clerk, after he both 'shouted instructions at him' and then wrote them down, was met with the forlorn response that 'I can't hear and I can't read'.[63] Even in his failure to vote, the report represented an ordinary citizen engaging in election politics despite significant personal issues. His effort, despite eventually being unable to successfully cast his vote, was another example presented to readers of a citizen who, through the efforts taken to try and engage in politics, was worthy of attention and praise.

Other's electoral efforts were similarly celebrated. A front page of the *Mirror* in late-January 1906, for example, was dedicated to a resident of Ipswich who was credited as 'the first voter at the first polling of the elections', and whose arrival at the polling office was 'specially' recorded by the newspaper.[64] Other Edwardian citizens were reported to be actively volunteering their services for the wider election cause, with mixed results. For instance, the *Daily Express* in 1906 featured election 'Humours and Misadventures' which highlighted some of the ways in which ordinary people were contributing to the ongoing campaign. One individual attempted to offer lifts to voting strangers caught in the rain, but was ultimately 'unable' due to the limits imposed by the election's bribery laws. Another had far less innocent intentions. He, who the article described as the 'wily one', was reported to have met a fellow elector at a train station and delayed him in friendly conversation long enough for the polls to close and thus not allow the arriving individual to vote for his, rival, candidate.[65] The stranger's victorious declaration 'next election, I think' was less earnest than the unlucky car driver or the early voter mentioned elsewhere, but all three people were equally highlighted by the *Express* as 'humorous' examples of ordinary citizens who were taking the time to engage in the election.

There were also individuals who engaged in even more unusual election behaviour. An 'election anecdote' published in the *Mirror* in January 1906 told of a butcher in an anonymous village who was 'a strong Tory'. Upon serving a Liberal-supporting women who had entered his shop asking for a sheep's head, he told her the best way ensure the sheep's head she purchased was Liberal; 'just take the brains out... needless to say (claimed the writer) he has lost a customer'.[66] While there were no other articles that featured quite the same level of election eccentricity, the story of the political butcher mirrored much of the same emphases seen in the profiles of ordinary and extraordinary everyman involvement in elections. It showcased how politics was not detached from everyman life. Rather, it was something with which ordinary people could engage in a variety of ways that were both serious and humorous. In either case, whether helping others to the polling station or joking at another party's expense, it was behaviour which the new dailies represented as an acceptable and noteworthy part of election practice. Even the saboteur at the train station was not criticised. Rather, he was 'wily', as opposed to unruly like those who attacked property and people at election meetings. The significance of this was to further situate election politics as represented in the new dailies as enjoyable events where people could engage in disruptive behaviour alongside actions of support and enthusiasm.

Seen together, these new daily profiles of the political actions of citizens – ranging across all four elections and including behaviour such as good-hearted support, singular determination when voting, and humorous acts of sabotage – showcased the various ways in which the imagined everyman could engage with general elections throughout the Edwardian period. These methods of engagement included 'everyman' across a wide variety of age groups, as well as people who were shown getting out of hospital beds in order to cast their votes. Through this inclusion of differently aged citizens and within the limits of the broader everyman identity, the political arena was shown to be welcoming to large numbers of the British public. This was especially the case due to the emphasis on both the very young and the very old; virtually any age was permitted within the everyman election culture which the new dailies conveyed through their coverage.

Moreover, the inclusion of disabled voters shown to be struggling from beds or wheelchairs to cast their votes was a further emphasis on the inclusiveness of elections. If these individuals could vote, then almost any other everyman could as well. Interestingly, those visual profiles also featured the voters receiving help from a variety of other citizens: police-officers, fellow voters, charitable passers-by. Rather than demeaning the physically disabled electors, however, these images represented the voting process as one defined by communal support; voters receiving support and encouragement from their fellow everyman. The representations of supportive voters went beyond the assistance to those in wheelchairs. Groups of people were shown giving (or at least trying to give) lifts in their motor vehicles to fellow voters to ensure they got swiftly and safely to their polling stations. These good Samaritans were not exceptions. Instead, their friendly actions and approachable demeanours helped to further suggest just how open and inclusive the act of voting was for the archetypal 'everyman' who was reading one of the three election-time new dailies. Regardless of age or distance from a polling station, the new dailies reported on an election environment where most people who were eligible to vote supported each other in the process of exercising their democratic rights.

The key underlying principle behind this broader representation of voting citizens was that voting was an attainable right, but this did not belittle the act of voting itself. The implicit importance of the vote was woven into the reports of the schoolchildren creating their own hustings and the patient discharged patient struggling into the taxi to head to vote; the extent of the inclusivity stressed the importance of casting one's vote. It cannot be ignored, once again, that this power could not be used by everyone in British society. The *Mirror* included an article in mid-January 1906 which quoted a 'specialist' – a Dr Forbes Wilmslow, quite possibly the same Dr Forbes Wilmslow who had involved themselves within the Jack the Ripper case – warning of the high risk of 'injurious and pernicious effect of the excitement of politics upon a woman's brain'. The other words used to simultaneously define and discourage women who were participating in the hustings – 'lose her reason... wreck her life... hysterical' – were a stark reminder to readers, and to the later historian, that there were those not included within the new dailies' inclusive representations of everyman election politics.[67]

The paradox within the new dailies' articulated vision of election politics – within which millions of British citizens had a powerful and easy-to-access role within political culture, but within crude parameters of gender and social behaviour – was outlined within this one copy of the *Mirror.* In the same edition which featured the warning of female election behaviour lunacy on the previous page, the paper explicitly outlined and promoted the 'Power of the Vote' which the everyman possessed; 'the vote is a thing of such great and splendid power... vote early and vote often'.[68]

The same day as the *Mirror* proclaimed the voting power with which Edwardian everyman should engage as early and frequently as possible, the *Express* featured an article which represented one of many 'Typical Constituencies' and the ways that, as this chapter has discussed, elections were represented as part of the day-to-day lives of their readers;

> Pasted on the plate-glass windows of a public house in High Street, Deptford, are two startling placards. One of them... exhorts the local elector to vote for Vivian, the Liberal candidate. The other sets out in attractive fashion the programme of a forthcoming series of prize-fights.[69]

Much like that London establishment's window, the new dailies featured content in which the elections of the Long Edwardian period were portrayed as a noteworthy and entertaining part of many of their reader's day-to-day lives. Politics became part of the paper's broader human-interest content and, in the process, further highlighted how readily many of their readers could and should engage with politics as part of their daily lives. Thanks particularly to amusing connections made by various companies between election news and their products, politics, and elections, in particular, became something which was situated within lived experiences of lower-middle-class daily life, such as shopping, eating, and drinking. Rather than specialist news content, elections could be understood and enjoyed by an everyman reader reading almost any page of an election-edition new daily. It was connected to people and products which resonated with the lived experiences of millions. It was this open access of political information that contributed to the election competitions, which encouraged the readers whom were included and amused by the references to an everyday, everyman political culture of which they were a part to put their skills to the test. Similar to how the public house window in Deptford situated the 1906 election alongside prize fights, the new dailies situated elections as being as entertaining and open to audience opinion as popular sport or a prize draw.

The collective significance of the above-discussed examples of the new dailies' everyday election coverage, and their promotion of the political everyman, was the extent to which they connected election proceedings to the kinds of people who made up most of their readerships. There was a repeated emphasis on the significance of the imagined 'everyman' within Edwardian political culture, and just how readily and enjoyably an everyman could flex their political muscle. Ultimately, it was the public from whom the prospective candidates needed support in order to win. This power was represented to readers of all three new dailies. The *Mirror* featured a particularly prominent display of the political power of the public in a double-page photographic feature which highlighted the range of people from whom politicians were speaking to guarantee their success at the polls: crowds of workers in Matlock; farmhands gathering to ask questions of their local candidate; children eager to learn more.[70]

These ordinary people – symbolic of the imagined everyman – were represented as the holders of political power. Indeed, as has been mentioned earlier in this book, parties across the Long Edwardian political spectrum were increasingly articulating election appeals towards a growingly mass, lower-middle and working-class electorate. What the next chapter will explore, therefore, is how voices from within three political parties – Liberal, Labour, and Conservative – reacted to the growth and consolidation of this new mass press. Drawing from archival discoveries documented from the launch of the first new daily to the end of peacetime, the next chapter paints a complex picture of the value placed on the new dailies by political organisations that, in theory, were seeking much the same 'man in the street' so successfully included within the new dailies' coverage of Long Edwardian elections.

Notes

1 'Saturday is the Last Day', *Daily Mail* 18 January 1906, p. 10.
2 'Another £50 Prize', *Daily Mirror* 17 January 1906, p. 5.
3 'Readers of the "Daily Mail" Invited to Forecast the Results', *Daily Mail* 29 September 1900, p. 7.
4 Stephanie Rains, 'Going in for Competitions', *Media History* 21, no. 2 (3 April 2015): 139, https://doi.org/10.1080/13688804.2014.995611.
5 Graham Law and Matthew Sterenberg, 'Old v. New Journalism and the Public Sphere; or, Habermas Encounters Dallas and Stead', *19: Interdisciplinary Studies in the Long Nineteenth Century* 1, no. 16 (22 March 2013): 10, https://doi.org/10.16995/ntn.657; Williams, *Read All About It! A History of the British Newspaper*, 127.
6 '£10,000 Flight', *Daily Mail* 17 November 1906, p. 5.

7 'How I Flew to Manchester', *Daily Mail* 29 April 1910, p. 8.
8 Rains, 'Going in for Competitions', 140.
9 Throughout this chapter, the words 'advertisements' and 'adverts' will be used interchangeably to refer to the same items of newspaper content.
10 'Special Election Result', *Daily Mirror* 9 December 1910, p. 11.
11 Ibid.
12 'Political Notes: Which will you Vote for?', *Daily Mail* 12 January 1906, p. 8.
13 'Always in Power: No Election Necessary', *Daily Mirror* 17 January 1910, p. 2.
14 *Daily Mirror* 20 January 1910, p. 10.
15 Ibid., p. 13.
16 *Daily Express* 26 January 1906, p. 3.
17 Ibid., p. 6.
18 *Daily Express* 27 January 1906, p. 3.
19 *Daily Express* 22 January 1906, p. 7.
20 *Daily Mail* 15 January 1906, p. 8.
21 *Daily Mail* 18 January 1906, p. 4.
22 'Vote! Vote!! Vote!!!', *Daily Mail* 17 January 1906, p. 10.
23 Ibid.
24 Ibid.
25 'Fair Trade and Protection to Customers', *Daily Express* 16 January 1906, p. 6.
26 'The Protection Candidate', *Daily Mail* 17 January 1906, p. 4.
27 'The Real Home Rule Question', *Daily Mail* 23 January 1906, p. 10.
28 'Cope's Bond of Union: Chinese 'slave' endorsement', *Daily Express* 31 January 1906, p. 2.
29 'The Voice of the People', *Daily Mail* 20 January 1910, p. 8.
30 *Daily Mirror* 2 February 1910, p. 11.
31 *Daily Mail* 6 December 1910, p. 9.
32 *Daily Mail* 9 December 1910, p. 7.
33 'Political Notes', *Daily Mail* 16 January 1906, p. 4.
34 *Daily Express* 23 January 1906, p. 3.
35 'A Message from Birmingham', *Daily Mail* 22 January 1906, p. 4.
36 Erika Rappaport, *Shopping for Pleasure: Women in the Making of London's West End* (Princeton, NJ: Princeton University Press, 2001), 143.
37 Peter Gurney, *The Making of Consumer Culture in Modern Britain* (London: Bloomsbury Academic, 2017), 75.
38 'Always in Power', *Daily Mirror* 17 January 1910, p. 2.
39 'Referendum', *Daily Mirror* 8 December 1910, p. 13.
40 'Vote for Camp Coffee', *Daily Mirror* 9 December 1910, p. 2.
41 'The Women Behind the Vote', *Daily Express* 17 January 1906, p. 4.
42 Ibid.
43 *Daily Mirror* 13 January 1906, p. 3.
44 Ibid., p. 4.
45 'First Lady Voter', *Daily Mirror* 17 January 1906, p. 5.
46 Bingham and Conboy, *Tabloid Century: The Popular Press in Britain, 1896 to the Present*, 131.
47 See Mari Takayanagi, 'Women and the Vote: The Parliamentary Path to Equal Franchise, 1918–28', *Parliamentary History* 37, no. 1 (February 2018): 168–85, https://doi.org/10.1111/1750-0206.12344.

48 Jacky Bratton, *The Making of the West End Stage: Marriage, Management and the Mapping of Gender in London, 1830–1870* (Cambridge: Cambridge University Press, 2011); Rob Lewis, '"Our Lady Specialists at Pikes Lane": Female Spectators in Early English Professional Football, 1880–1914', *The International Journal of the History of Sport* 26, no. 15 (December 2009): 2161–81, https://doi.org/10.1080/09523360903367651; Catriona M. Parratt, 'Little Means or Time: Working–Class Women and Leisure in Late Victorian and Edwardian England', *International Journal of Phytoremediation* 21, no. 1 (1998): 22–53, https://doi.org/10.1080/09523369808714027; Lynn Walker, 'Vistas of Pleasure: Women Consumers and Urban Space in the West End of London, 1850–1900', in *Women in the Victorian Art World*, ed. Clarissa Campbell Orr (Manchester: Manchester University Press, 1995), 70–88; Jean Williams, *A Game for Rough Girls? A History of Women's Football in Britain* (London: Routledge, 2003), 25–44.

49 Sarah Richardson, 'Parliament as Viewed Through a Woman's Eyes: Gender and Space in the 19th-Century Commons', *Parliamentary History* 38, no. 1 (1 February 2019): 119–34, https://doi.org/10.1111/1750-0206.12416.

50 Henry Miller, 'The 1910 Petitions on Women's Suffrage: An Unofficial Referendum – Committees – UK Parliament', UK Parliament Committees, 2017, https://committees.parliament.uk/committee/326/petitions-committee/news/99171/the-1910-petitions-on-womens-suffrage-an-unofficial-referendum/ [accessed 10 March 2021].

51 Vessey, 'Words as Well as Deeds: The Popular Press and Suffragette Hunger Strikes in Edwardian Britain'.

52 *Daily Mirror* 13 January 1906, p. 4.

53 Ibid., p. 3.

54 *Daily Mirror* 23 January 1906, p. 3.

55 'The Gentle Art of Heckling', *Daily Mail* 11 October 1900, p. 4.

56 Gurney, *The Making of Consumer Culture in Modern Britain*, 63; Trygve R. Tholfsen, 'The Transition to Democracy in Victorian England', *International Review of Social History* 6, no. 2 (18 August 1961): 226–28, https://doi.org/10.1017/S0020859000001838.

57 'I am the Man in the Street', *Daily Express* 12 January 1906, p. 4.

58 Ibid.

59 'Humours of a School Election', *Daily Mirror* 5 December 1910, p. 3.

60 'Election Pitfalls', *Daily Mirror* 3 December 1910, p. 3.

61 *Daily Mail* 17 October 1900, p. 5.

62 *Daily Mirror* 17 January 1910, p. 9.

63 'Election Items', *Daily Mail* 9 October 1900, p. 5.

64 *Daily Mirror* 13 January 1906, p. 1.

65 'Some Election News Stories', *Daily Express* 13 January 1906, p. 4.

66 'An Election Anecdote', *Daily Mirror* 16 January 1906, p. 7.

67 *Daily Mirror* 15 January 1906, p. 5.

68 Ibid., p. 6.

69 'Some Typical Constituencies', *Daily Express* 15 January 1906, p. 4.

70 *Daily Mirror* 3 December 1910, pp. 10–11.

4 Their Views and Ours

Politicians and the New Dailies

As Chapters 2 and 3 have explored, the new dailies of the Long Edwardian period represented an important and innovative form of mass political communication. The ways that all three newspapers used sensationalism and personalisation within their reporting of political events increasingly portrayed the political process as an exciting, dramatic, and accessible part of the 'everyman' lives of millions of their large and primarily lower-middle-class readerships. Their potential to communicate politics to unprecedented numbers of people and place those same people at the heart of the political process, meant that the new dailies marked a hugely significant development in the history of British politics, the British political press, and British democracy.

This chapter explores the varied ways in which Edwardian Britain's three major political parties, faced with this new potential form of mass political communication, responded to its potential. The differences in reactions across each party, drawn what has remained within both the central party archives and other related collections outlined in Chapter 1, spoke of broader attitudes within each party to the potential, or worthiness, of using popular newspapers for the purposes of political communication. This chapter breaks down these reactions into each of the three principal parties in Britain, looking at how voices within (in respective order) Labour, the Conservative, and the Liberal parties discussed and debated the new dailies and their potential impact on the political status quo. How members of each party reacted, so this chapter argues, sheds significant light on the histories of each party by seeing their responses to the new dailies as representative of broader political attitudes towards both popular culture and the wants of amass electorate that, outwardly at least, seemed increasingly central to the ideology and proposed policy of all three parties.

DOI: 10.4324/9781003254263-4

Labour[1]: Yellow Dailies

The rise and rapid consolidation of the new dailies ran near-parallel to the rise of the British Labour Party. From an electorally unassuming inception in 1900, Labour concluded the Long Edwardian period as a major force in British politics. By the end of the period, they had supplanted the Irish Nationalists as Britain's third-largest party in terms of votes received. They had also served as a significant voice in Parliament by supporting the governing Liberals, whose earlier pact with the party in 1906 contributed to influencing policy decisions that explicitly addressed concerns that were raised by Labour MPs. Moreover, their political emphasis was (perhaps unsurprisingly) on trying to better represent the interests of Britain's poorer classes: populations that were similar to the primary readers, and ready consumers, of the new dailies. This broad correlation between the intended audiences of both the new dailies and Labour was prevalent across Labour reactions to the new dailies and was a likely contributor to the fact that Labour, more than the other parties, reacted strongly to the rise of a newspaper press which sold particularly well to the man in the street. These reactions can be retrospectively divided into two distinct groups and expose Labour's complicated relationship with popular media as a political medium prior to their growing acceptance of its potential after the end of World War I, as noted by Laura Beers.

The emergence of the new dailies was met with a considerable amount of hostility from voices across the Labour party, including those at both a higher institutional level and among the party's grassroots supporters. Initially, it is easy to understand the place of those reactions take in existing narratives concerning the British left's long-running issues with popular media. However, what is striking to see is the specific nature of the hostility shown towards these newspapers, in particular, both within private written correspondence between party agents and political writings and editorials in left-wing periodicals of the period.

The hostility shown by Labour activists and supporters towards the new dailies across this period can be collected into two broad categories. The first of these thematic bands of criticism related to the overly commercial approach to journalism that these new daily newspapers were taking. Their cheap price (the *Daily Mail* was, for instance, sold at one-sixth the price of *The Times*) and prominent featuring of flashy advertisements for consumer goods were very likely principal factors in the word 'capitalist' being used as shorthand in much of the discussion about these new newspapers.

Closer inspection shows that the reactions to these new papers as 'capitalist' had a uniqueness specific to the nature of these specific paper's content. For example, surviving letters that were sent to the Labour party secretary Ramsey Macdonald highlight how the rise of these new, cheap mass newspapers had struck a distinct chord of discomfort among elements of the party's support base. Most notably, a private contributor named Gilmour Stephenson wrote several times to the party, stressing how the unique cheapness of these new 'capitalist' newspapers posed a profound threat to the Labour cause. By further labelling these papers as 'halfpenny' publications, the problem they caused was specific to their affordability and, thus, how easily available these publications were to the mass, lower-earning public.[2] Moreover, he noted that these papers, being defined by their attention to advertising interests and low prices, failed to carry positive messages about Labour, in contrast to positive reports on both the Liberals and the Conservatives. Mr Stephenson echoed some months later by another private citizen writing to MacDonald from Nottingham.[3] Attached to these letters were cuttings from popular 'halfpenny' newspapers explicitly praising the other two parties, so included as to highlight the relative absence of positive coverage of Labour within this new newspaper market.[4]

This concern over the cheapness and overt 'capital' presence on the pages of these newspapers was also reflected in Labour Party reactions published in the socialist press. For example, the *Labour Leader* mentioned the new daily popular press on multiple occasions and always with the same criticisms and reservations about its commercial nature. Much like the private concerns sent to the party, public criticisms of this new press rarely referred to their titles but instead labelled them 'capitalist'. These same papers were accused of writing 'insidious attacks'[5] on the Labour party and movement. On the occasions when either of the two new dailies are specifically named, it is in relation to a particular disservice that publication had done to either the *Leader* or the labour movement as a whole.

For example, the naming of the *Daily Mail* related to a supposed scandal relating to their coverage of certain motor cars. Accused of including advertising 'puffs' from salespeople for certain cars and then pocketing profit from future sales, the critique of the *Mail* was intrinsically linked to its identity as a commercial or 'capitalist' publication, as it was embroiled in dodgy dealings with business and advertising interests.[6] This theme of the blurring of business and journalistic professions was picked up by other left-wing titles such as the *Cooperative News*. The paper published an editorial two months prior to the

Leader's 'dodge' article that attacked 'advertisements' and 'vested interests' as being the sole concerns of new generations of popular newspapers.[7] Both in public and in private, therefore, sections of Labour were reacting to the new popular daily press as an entity defined by its attention to advertising and its perceived cheap, commercial approach to journalism.

Twinned with this focus on 'capital' was a concern over this new press's moral worth, and particularly its perceived attention to truthfulness. Alongside references to the 'capitalist' press, there are references to this new press as being 'yellow'. This term, a reference both to the sensational penny papers of mid-Victorian America[8] and a derogatory comment on the quality of paper used to print cheap dailies, becomes interchangeable shorthand along with 'capitalist' to refer to the same sorts of newspapers. Its frequent use underlined how the surviving Labour reactions to the new dailies were not only concerned with the paper's attention to capital and commercial interests; they were convinced it was actively dishonest.

The nature of this 'dishonesty' had two distinct levels. On one level, the new dailies were accused of lying in the form of their attention to personal scandal and outrageous, arguably libellous claims of personal or institutional wrongdoing. One particular dismissive article in the *Leader* detailing the 'yellow' press's unimpeded printing of "baseless" charges and rumours ended with a statement that gets to the heart of many of Labour's reactions to the new dailies:

> The publishing of scandalous reports as statements of fact is at all times an abominable practice, and ought to be put a stop to; but if the yellow press in this country (Britain) were punished every time it published scurrilous unverified rumours, well, where would it be?[9]

Besides the obvious, sarcastic dismissal of the new dailies as reliant on these 'scurrilous' types of articles, this reaction goes deeper than a hatred of lies and indicates quite why so much of Labour and the wider left were so hostile towards this new press. Going back to the traditions (and large circulations) of the unstamped and radical presses of the early and pre-Victorian periods,[10] the British left had long imagined an ideal newspaper press as being an educator through which workers and the wider working- and lower-middle classes could gain knowledge and attain self-betterment. Indeed, the British radical presses of the earlier nineteenth centuries had been active parts of wider social and political movements that were fighting for the betterment of the politically underrepresented British public.[11] This educationalist and radical tradition lay at the heart of Labour's negative reactions to the new dailies.

First, the new dailies' cheap prices and significant presence of 'capitalist' advertising for everyday products meant that they were attempting to, and succeeding in, appealing to mass, lower-middle and working-class, urban sections of the British public. It was these same broad demographics that the emerging Labour party also wished to communicate with. As Labour imagined both itself and the press as educational entities, these new dailies were essentially lecturing to similar types of people to whom they also wished to lecture. These 'halfpenny' papers were a direct rival in Labour's mission to educate the wider British public.

Second, as well as trying to speak to the same groups of people, the new dailies were speaking to them about topics that were thoroughly at odds with early Labour's understanding of both the role of the press and the needs and wants of working-class people. Some of the core aspects of the New Journalism and the new popular dailies were particularly at odds with some of the central tenets of early British socialism; this kind of journalism served to entertain, not to educate or reform. Additionally, the prominence of sports coverage in the new dailies troubled the early left due to many sports' close ties to the socialist vices of alcohol consumption and gambling. Long editorials in leftist publications such as one entitled 'Should Football be Stopped?'[12] underlined the broader negativity many in Labour held towards the content so readily discussed by the new popular dailies. Whenever these core features of the new dailies were discussed in left-wing publications of the period, from football to the consumption of beer,[13] the same animosity was present.

In summary, the reactions of Labour to these new dailies were consistently hostile. On the rare occasions that one of the papers was cited by name, it was in relation to an error they had committed, whether dubious financial links to advertisers or, as seen in a brief exchange between the *Daily Express* and the *Leader's* editor John Bruce Glasier, their general mistreatment of socialism on their pages.[14] The other times that they merited reactions categorised them as a 'yellow' and 'capitalist' enemy. By speaking to lower-middle and working-class audiences through their cheap pricing and by prioritising stories around crime, sensation and sport, they were the antithesis of what Labour expected and desired from a newspaper. They were something to judge, ridicule, and oppose.

Yet, bizarrely, at the same time as being an enemy to Labour, the new dailies were seen as something to copy and repurpose for the benefit of the movement. They were the enemy, but one from whom lessons needed to be learned. As was highlighted above, the rise of the new popular daily press generated very troubled responses from across both the Labour party and the wider Labour movement. It was seen largely as a hostile force against their cause, particularly as it was appealing to similar groups of people that Labour wished to reach. Within this hostile reaction, however, was a parallel desire to repurpose the new dailies for the benefit of Labour. As hostile as Labour was, there was also a strong sense of appreciation for the potential political power of such a press if it were in the hands of socialists.

For example, the same letters written that were bemoaning the dangers of the halfpenny daily press also implored the party to take steps to create a halfpenny daily newspaper of their own. To refer back to Gilmour Stephenson, for example, their written concerns of the halfpenny press also came with a cry that it was 'necessary' that Labour set up its own paper that was sold as regularly and cheaply as the halfpenny press; the party needed a direct competitor to the new dailies to counter their negative impact on their mass audiences of working-class readers.[15] Furthermore, the steady growth of Labour victories during the 1906 general election saw Ramsey Macdonald receive multiple letters from various party agents and supporters stating the urgent need for a daily Labour publication, in order to build on the electoral success.[16]

This same sentiment was echoed across the same left-wing press that were so vehemently opposed to the new dailies' content and journalistic approach. The *Leader*, for example, ran multiple articles calling for a socialist daily newspaper that appealed to the 'man on the street' who so regularly consumed the new dailies.[17] These articles would also cite the success of other left-wing daily newspapers in both Europe and the United States, so as to highlight the existing lack of an equivalent in Britain, as well as the popular success that such a title would likely achieve if ever brought into being.[18]

These reactions from across the party calling for a socialist popular daily were also of keen interest to both the party elites and leading figures in allied movements, particularly the Trade Union Congress. As was noted in Brown's chapter on early Labour and the press, Labour and its allies strived for years to create a national newspaper operating in the interest of Labour, including attempts to purchase the existing *Daily News* and the disastrous, one-week existence of a paper entitled

The Majority.[19] While Brown notes the party's eventual emphasis on a national daily newspaper, it was not always the case. Initially, it had been the Parliamentary Committee of the TUC which proposed a daily Labour paper in 1903,[20] and it was only after the 1906 general election that the central party moved away from its initial preference of a cheaper, easier to maintain weekly publication.[21] Ramsey Macdonald, who later would be among the leading party figures pushing for the creation of a daily, initially replied to the TUC's 1903 resolution by stating that "daily papers must be local" due to the "impossibility" of getting a daily from one end of the country to the other.[22]

This steady development in Labour's more positive reactions to the new dailies and their potential political usefulness indicates how the hostility towards the newspapers' content and purpose was gradually joined by an appreciation of the unique power that a cheap, daily newspaper would have with regards to furthering the national Labour mission. The concerns over the practicality of daily distribution and the cost and manner of setting one up gradually receded as a daily's potential worth grew in the minds of the party elite. However, while misplaced individual concerns that 'dailies had to be local' soon subsided, a profound ideological confusion continued to define Labour's understandings of the new dailies throughout the Long Edwardian period: even after they attempted to create a new daily of their own.

A Red Daily

In October 1912, a new newspaper was launched in Britain. This newspaper, to be printed and sold daily at halfpenny an issue and eight pages in length, was specifically created to appeal to the sorts of news-reading audiences that had been buying the new dailies. Its pricing, visual layout and editorial emphasis on human interest sensation made it a direct competitor to the new dailies. This particular newspaper, however, was unique. This new newspaper was called the *Daily Citizen* and was created, financed, and ran by the recently founded Labour Party. Labour launched the *Citizen* to try and communicate with the mass audiences that were regularly buying the new popular press: a direct attempt to try and capture the success of the new dailies and their potential to communicate to large readerships. Ultimately, the *Daily Citizen* survived for a little over two years, during which time it hit a peak daily circulation of approximately a quarter-of-a-million copies. Its brief existence has been previously discussed by historians in very brief detail[23] and in reference to a small part of its content,[24] and the paper's eventual demise has long been dismissed as a simple lack of revenue and the crippling costs of the daily newspaper business.[25]

While it failed in its intended mission, its existence offers a unique insight into the early Labour movement and its complex relationship with both the popular newspaper industry and the mass, working-class public that it claimed to naturally represent. Across the pages of the *Citizen* can be seen an ideological struggle at the heart of the early British left. By trying to speak to the readers of the new dailies, Labour found itself at odds with much of the traditional British left's understanding of the nature of journalism, the purpose of the party, and the lives of the workers they wanted to politically represent. Far from being a forgotten, fleeting experiment, the *Daily Citizen* can and should be seen as a key case study of the British left and its long-standing and often problematic relationships with popular media and the mainstream public.

Due to its desire to speak to the 'man on the street', much of its content mirrored that seen in the popular new dailies of the same period. This attention to the 'human interest' and the news genres explored so effectively by early New Journalism innovators such as George Newnes and Alfred Harmsworth resulted in the *Daily Citizen* behaving across significant sections of each edition as a 'yellow' daily that prioritized sensation, scandal and entertainment in its coverage of news.

One of the most prominent ways in which the *Citizen* seemed to attempt behaviour of a popular, 'yellow' daily was how it reported on crime and, in particular, violent crimes, as well as summaries from trial proceedings. Salacious coverage of violent or shocking crime was one of the bedrocks of the British New Journalism, most notoriously seen in Stead's 'The Maiden Tribute of Modern Babylon' discussed in Chapter 1. While nothing on the pages of the *Citizen* reached those levels of controversy, they were similar in their evocative and dramatically headlined reports of horrible crimes.

One crime topic that the *Citizen* showed particular interest in was the issue of 'white slavery': the trafficking of women and girls that was a recurring and heavily racialized popular sensation before and during the Long Edwardian era.[26] This topic was explored in several different ways, but with a consistent emphasis on the unsavoury intentions of those working in the slave trade. One such article, dated from 1 January 1913, focused on the danger faced by two young girls leaving their homes in Salford to live alone in London. Headlined '*Young Girls in Peril: Narrow Escape from White Slavery*', it explored the risks of running away from home due to the 'dangers of the streets' that faced innocent youths on the streets of the capital. Specifically, it told of a network of people, including a woman offering free taxi rides and 'two foreigners' who tried to ensnare the two girls before the arrival of police, and how astute interventions from alert, caring members of the public, scared them into running away.[27] The decision to describe two of the involved by their non-British identity is particularly noteworthy as an additional link between the *Daily Citizen* and the new dailies, whose jingoistic attitudes to nation and the Empire had become one of their defining features of their reporting on the Second Boer War, as mentioned in Chapter 2.

Another white slavery article, published in the same week, outlined guidelines for other young girls who the newspaper saw as running the risk of falling for the '*White Slave Traps*' that had been attempted on the girls from Salford. Readers, and specifically young girls, were warned that they;

> should never speak to strangers... should never ask the way of any but officials on duty, such as policemen... should never loiter or stand about alone in the street... should never stay to help a woman who apparently faints at their feet in the street, and should immediately call a policeman to her aid.[28]

Later that same month, another white slavery article was published in the *Citizen*, this time detailing the '*Attempted Drugging of a Girl*'. The 'traffickers... these pests to society' tried to drug and kidnap a woman 'employed at a well-known Oxford Street drapery establishment' before escaping the attentions of nearby police. This account was made especially shocking both due to the nature of the intended victim – a woman of established society, not a young runaway – and its reporting as 'a bare-faced attempt to drug her in the street (using) an open jar, from which pungent and acrid fumes arose'.[29] This time, the threat was not the shady backstreets, but broad daylight on one of London's most historic and prestigious streets. These dramatic reconstructions of 'white slavery crimes' are a particularly strong case study of the *Citizen's* attempted emulation of new daily crime reporting. Not only was it reported on similarly salacious crimes, but it was evoking the same kinds of emotional emphases: helpless young white women, predatory non-British agents, and frightful warnings of the risks and ruin facing the unprepared on an everyday street.

The *Daily Citizen's* sensationalized representations of crime were part of a wider focus on 'human interest' news content: stories that focused on emotive language of matters relating to events and situations that everyday readers of popular papers could better relate to. These human interests were varied in topic, but shared a sensationalist approach to the headlining and construction of the story, where the primary intention of the article was to provoke an instant, emotional response. One such manifestation of human-interest sensation was reporting of high-society scandal. One such example reported on a road accident involving the wife of Winston Churchill, which was described as a 'motor smash' that injured her with 'broken glass'.[30] The fact that the report under this dramatic headline stated her wounds were very minor (a 'slight cut') further underlines how the principal aim of the piece, considering the initial conclusions that are implied from its outlandish headline, was to generate an instinctive, rather than a considered, reader response. In another, a front-page piece from June 1913 concerning the fate of Captain Scott and his Antarctic exploration team refers to the 'Tent of Death' as the scene of their deaths, and advertises how the tent will be on show at an exhibition in Earl's Court later that year.[31] Again, the coverage of high society drama is constructed in very dramatic terms, with headlines that seem to deliberately invite shocked, emotional reactions.

Coverage of high society drama was complemented with reports of drama of the 'everyday' stories more closely connected to the lives of the people that Labour wanted to be reading their popular daily newspaper. One of the most striking examples of this everyday drama was reports of sudden deaths. Much as with its coverage of high society scandal, the *Citizen's* handling of domestic, everyday tragedies was primarily framed around scenarios designed to provoke primarily emotional responses. The types of intended emotional responses to these stories could vary considerably.

On the one hand, stories such as one concerning a housewife 'worked to death' seemed principally to wish to provoke heartbreak. Such stories detailed the good nature of the victim, such as this particular woman's 'devoted and cheerful' attitude to her 'exceptionally hard life', which comprised having to run a house of four young children and care for, as well as work in the place of, her consumption-afflicted husband. This idealistic vision of caring, traditional household woman is then dramatically contrasted with the events that caused death:

> Up to Saturday last she had attended to her frames in the cotton factory with unwavering and unfailing regularity from six o'clock in the morning until 5.30 in the evening... Returning, she put her children to bed and soon afterwards her husband had a sudden seizure.
>
> She was hurrying to the bedroom when she was heard to exclaim, "Oh, my head". Collapsing entirely, she fell across her husband on the bed and passed away.[32]

This extract, indicative of similar reports throughout other editions of the *Citizen,* constructs the everyday tragedy of a woman who died due to 'heart failure brought on by overwork' into a short story. By focusing on the emotive qualities of the deceased and then depicting her death as a dramatic climax (complete with last words), the news report takes on qualities that could easily be attributed to a piece of literary or theatrical fiction. The focus was deliberately and overwhelmingly on the emotive elements of the story – its empathy and its shock reveal – and articulated news less as a recounting of facts, and more as a theatrical reconstruction.

This emphasis on the dramatization of everyday news was also used to explore or heighten the less serious or even openly comedic aspects of domestic tragedy. One such example, headlined 'Death Bed Mishap' and concerning a dying widow in Florence, stated:

> The woman was dying, and a priest was administering the last sacrament to her in the presence of about 80 relatives and friends, as is the custom in the district. The bedroom, which was on the first floor of the house, was packed to overflowing.
>
> While those assembled were praying the floor gave way, and all the people, including the dying woman, were precipitated to the floor below.[33]

Again, a story of household death is constructed in the *Citizen* as a dramatic story. In his case however, as in others, the story is made to be light-hearted, from the 'mishap' headline to the suddenness of the collapse. The relative absence of detail post-collapse, such as details of specific numbers killed or injured, further emphasizes how everyday tragedy in the *Daily Citizen* served a primary role of entertaining, as much as informing, the reader.

This interest in reader entertainment is also very apparent in one of the *Daily Citizen*'s most deliberate attempts to capture a new daily readership; its sports coverage. Coverage of sports, in particular, football, had become a defining aspect of the new dailies and the New Journalism as a whole by the beginning of the twentieth century.[34] The particular dedication to football across large sections of the British press spoke considerably of the sport's increasingly prominent place in British mass culture during the by the early twentieth century.[35] Particular newspapers, specifically elements of the daily evening press, prioritised football and sports coverage more generally as a key selling point to large audiences of lower-middle- and upper-working-class readers.[36] Even traditional newspapers such as *The Times,* albeit with a degree of hesitancy, had begun to include sports coverage by the beginning of the long-Edwardian era due to its undeniable mass popularity.[37] The *Citizen* seemed to fully appreciate the mass appeal of sports reports, and dedicated significant sections of every pre-war addition, often on its own page entitled 'Special Page of Sporting News' to cover news from cricket, horse racing, rugby and, most of all, football.

The most common sports articles in the *Citizen* were football match reports, which detailed the events of matches from across the country. It would often introduce its sports pages published during the football season was a 'League Review' or 'Football in Review', which would provide brief round-ups of games across the top two divisions. Headlines and sub-headings in the football reports seemed to pay particular attention to certain teams such as the London clubs Arsenal and Chelsea, the two Manchester clubs and other successful teams of the era such as Newcastle, Sunderland, and Everton. The emphasis of reports on the time's most successful and highest-profile football clubs strongly suggests the paper's eagerness to speak to the largest football-loving audience, by focusing its coverage on the teams that were likely to be the best-supported and most-discussed.

This attention by the *Citizen* on football's most popular elements was especially apparent in how it covered the Football Association (FA) Cup. The tournament, especially its latter stages, made news around the world, and both its prestige and mass appeal resulted in the *Citizen* giving the cup additional coverage outside of its sports section. While the early rounds of the cup would occasionally receive special attention, such as one sports page being retitled entirely to focus on 'Today's Cup Ties', the 1913 FA Cup Final was a standout example of the *Citizen's* attention to popular sports coverage.

The game, played between the First Division's top two teams Aston Villa and Sunderland, received multiple pages of dedicated coverage on both the day of, and the days after, the game. Full page profiles were provided of both teams, with photographs and illustrations of every member of the two squads with a brief description of their position on the field and their personal beginnings.[38] The game itself received a two-page spread in the first edition after the final was played, complete with a full-page cartoon which depicted the events of the game and accompanying speech bubbles speculating on what players and fans were saying at key points during the match.[39] In keeping with the *Citizen's* broader interest in the everyman, there was also attention paid to those who went to watch the game at London's Crystal Palace. Of particular prominence was a photograph taken of people sat watching the final in a tree overlooking the ground, the headline of which approved their 'Tree Top Enthusiasm'.[40]

The coverage of the 1913 FA Cup Final, with its attention to dramatic reconstruction, eye-grabbing headlines and visuals, and the everyman presence in the story, acts as an excellent microcosm of the broader ways in which the *Daily Citizen* strove to be a popular halfpenny daily. It presented news in ways as entertaining as they were informative, using language and visual elements that highlighted the dramatic and narrative elements of the news being presented. It was a concise and content-diverse newspaper that encapsulated many of the popular New Journalism innovations that had helped publications such as the *Mail* become such huge successes.

The problem that faced the *Citizen*, and a hugely significant reason why this Labour daily failed, was that this populist, 'yellow' journalism was not its whole identity. While the dailies it was clearly trying to emulate were consistent in their popular, New Journalism approach, the *Citizen* was not just a popular 'yellow' daily. It was also a 'red' daily: a socialist newspaper that, consistent with other left-wing publications of the period, was opposed to the very kind of press that it was so clearly trying to imitate. With the banner under every front-page reading 'Owned and Controlled by the Labour Movement', it was a daily reminder to readers that this was, above all else, a party-political newspaper. For all the attention to diverse New Journalism content, this was principally a political organ for the party to talk to a larger audience, and had been founded with this as its sole objective. In this context, the 'yellow' content sits uncomfortably alongside the more traditional socialist newspaper content that was also published in the *Daily Citizen*.

Understandably for a Labour newspaper, considerable space was set aside for matters concerning Labour politics. Page three of most pre-war editions of the citizen was set aside for 'Labour' news, with large sections entitled 'Labour at Home', 'Labour's Vision', and 'Labour Abroad'. These sections were comprised of articles, sometimes written by prominent member or associates of the party such as MPs and trade union leaders, detailing a proposed new Labour policy, or the party's stance on a new piece of government legislation. They would also provide sympathetic summaries of labourer disputes, outlining the reasons for the industrial action and providing readers with updates on ongoing struggles. One high-profile example of these kinds of reports was the paper's running coverage of striking London taxi drivers. The latter struggles of the 'taxi-cab war' received particular attention, and it, and other notable strikes, would occasionally make the front page.[41] Such occasions included a large miners' strike in early May 1913,[42] and a mass walkout in Belgium which was the first item of front-page news on the same day as the before-mentioned 1913 FA Cup Final.[43] The latter front-page story, coupled with the regular inclusion of the news section 'Labour Abroad' showed that the *Citizen* intended readers to have a global understanding of labour struggles, rather than just matters close to home. There was an assumption, or expectation, that its readers would want, or should want, to know about socialism as part of an internationalist understanding of working-class struggle, in addition to the messages included in the paper from domestic leaders of the labour movement.

This content differed considerably from much of the 'yellow' news contained in the *Citizen* as it was considerably more fact-driven, and less dependent on emotive language. For example, the large miner's strike on the front page of 3 May 1913 is reported as matter-of-fact, focusing on the numbers gathering to protest against non-unionist employees;

> In the Rhondda Valley...the strikers number over 11,000. This total includes nearly 7,000 men at the Tylerstown and Ferndale pits. There are nearly 12,000 men on strike in the Aberdale Valley, and of these 5,000 are at the Powell Duffryn and 5,000 at Nixon's Navigation.[44]

The story's more traditional and educationalist approach to journalism – a provision of factual details – is a sharp contrast to the popular content that is explored elsewhere in the paper. The different tone of this and other similarly 'red' articles is often made even more striking by being placed alongside sensationalist 'yellow' news. In the case of the mining strike, the story directly next to it showcases the other side to the *Citizen's* content;

REVOLVER DUEL IN TRAIN
Bandit's Encounter with Millionaire
A telegram from Kansas City gives particulars of one of the most daring and melodramatic hold-ups in American railway history.[45]

The most significant aspect of the *Citizen's* inclusion of both sensationalist and educationalist news material was not the diversity of subject matter, as one of the most successful aspects of popular newspapers was the breadth of content that they provided to readers.[46] Rather, it was that the two types of news were approached and represented in fundamentally different ways, using language and sometimes even formatting that spoke of two different newspaper traditions: that of a popular newspaper, and that of a traditional socialist newspaper.

This contrast of newspaper styles and approaches was thrown into even sharper contrast when different articles were discussing the same subject matter. This most noticeably occurred in the *Citizen*'s reporting on sports. Interspersed between the match reports, the photographs and the cartoons, articles would appear that offered an often self-labelled 'socialist' angle into the sport under discussion, most usually football. These included reports on the work of the London Playing Fields Society, who worked to provide sports pitches for Londoners,[47] as well as pieces educating readers on the 'joy of exercise' and why they (workers) should be trying to play more sport in their free time due to sport's real 'significance'.[48] One article also attacks the 'sordid commercialism' that it sees as part of the modern game, in response to a player moving to Blackburn Rovers for a transfer fee of £2,000, bemoaning how no man's skill at football should command such an investment.[49]

These types of articles sat uncomfortably next to the newspaper's more sensationalist sports coverage because they spoke of the *Daily Citizen*'s ideological similarity with the more traditional left-wing publications of its time. These titles, such as the *Labour Leader*, gave little-to-no attention to sport in their weekly content, and any inclusion of sport would focus on a negative aspect of that particular sport. Football was spoken of particularly negatively, due to its (according to one long read in an edition of the *Cooperative News*) negative influence on the moral character of the masses who watched it, as well as the sport's close ties to both gambling and the consumption of alcohol.[50] Therefore, throughout the multitudes of enthusiastic reports into popular sports, the *Daily Citizen* espoused a traditional, left-wing scepticism of popular sport, questioning the real moral and political value of one of its most discussed and, if wanting to be a popular daily, essential genres of news content.

This uncomfortable combination of populist enthusiasm and traditionalist scepticism was present in other sections of most editions of the *Daily Citizen*. For instance, attempts to mirror the women's sections of newspapers such as the *Daily Mail* contained long, moralising articles on certain aspects of popular culture. Most notably, a full-page spread was dedicated to the question 'Is Modern Dancing Decadent?' and strongly argued for;

> *a revival of the good, old-fashioned British dances...*
>
> *(and) I have no hesitation in denouncing in no uncertain terms the freak dances of to-day. Such dances as the Chicken Crawl and the Liverpool Lurch ought not to be tolerated anywhere. The danger is that once made popular in our music halls they find their way to the dancing hall.*[51]

Articles such as these, seen within both the context of the newspaper's broader duality of content and the attitudes espoused by its similarly left-wing contemporaries, indicate a broader ideological problem that hampered the *Daily Citizen* throughout much of its time in circulation. On the one hand, it included popular content on sensation and sport to try to behave like a popular daily, thus attracting similar numbers of readers as other popular new dailies. However, it never truly became a popular daily due to its persistent inclusion of traditional socialist understandings of what news content should be. The paper's backers seemed to understand that topics like sport, serialised crime and popular culture were genres of news that mass audiences wanted to read. However, it never seemed comfortable just speaking to these readers on their terms. To the leaders of the early Labour movement, a newspaper passed on appropriate knowledge; its job was to inform, not to entertain. It appreciated certain news genres were popular, which is why they were included. However, as was showcased in the criticisms of sport, the sudden switches between types of news language and the above-cited derision of popular sensations such as music-hall dances, it did not understand or appreciate their value to the people reading them.

The *Daily Citizen*, therefore, had a profound problem of identity. It struggled between trying to be a light-hearted daily, and wanting to be a serious, educationalist Labour paper. Its inclusion of popular content showcased many of the linguistic, narrative and visual innovations popularised so successfully by the new dailies, and demonstrated the party's determination to want to make a newspaper that spoke to a large audience of readers comprised primarily of Britain's lower-middle and working classes. However, it could not fully embrace this 'yellow' identity, thanks to deeply held beliefs across much of the early Labour movement concerning the journalistic merit of the types of news content and popular topics that were so regularly discussed in other popular dailies. This problematic duality in the *Citizen's* content and purpose was further compounded by how the paper represented the other popular newspapers that it was trying to emulate. The attitudes towards the press printed in the *Citizen* suggested that the problems that faced Labour's daily newspaper were also ones facing the movement as a whole. Principally, how to understand and appreciate the wants and interests of the mass, working public.

The *Daily Citizen* did not just publish occasional anti-press articles, however. Instead, it would dedicate a section at the bottom of page two of every pre-war edition to a section titled 'Their Views and Ours'. This section would be comprised of snippets taken from other newspapers, including frequent reference to the *Mail* and the *Express*, accompanied by a response from the *Citizen* mocking that paper's content;

> *"It is still possible to be a worker and a lady", says the Daily Sketch. Perish this foolish delusion!*[52]
> *"Take the Tube home", says the Daily Mail. To use as a garden hose, or what?*[53]
> *"Have you ever felt a desperate longing to get away from everything?", asks the Daily Mail. Often, but the ubiquity of our contemporary makes the longing futile.*[54]
> *"In politics we have working-class measures", says Reynold's. The Liberal imagination running riot.*[55]

These critiques, aimed at popular national publications of both Liberal and Conservative allegiance, served as a daily reminder of the Labour movement's low opinion of the popular press. It was a reminder that the movement as a whole understood mass-popular newspapers as dishonest, poor-quality publications that fed workers the wrong kind of journalistic diet. It was also a daily statement of the party's perceived superiority over the popular press, as they knew what workers really needed to read about in their daily newspaper. Workers should not be reading unintelligent newspapers such as the *Daily Mail* or *Reynold's*; they should be reading the higher-quality, informed *Daily Citizen*.

This daily stance taken in the *Citizen* exposed two fundamental flaws in the mind-set of the early labour movement. First, these regular reminders of the supposed unscrupulous or unintelligent nature of popular newspapers were being printed in their own take on a popular newspaper. By regularly mocking the entity they were demonstrably using as the *Citizen's* influence, they further enhanced the uncomfortable duality of the Labour daily's content, which was equally enthusiastic about, and entirely dismissive of, popular news content.

More than that, however, 'Their Views and Ours' spoke considerably of Labour's attitude towards the British mass public with whom they wished to engage. By launching a cheap, eight-page daily, and including sensationalist and popular news content, they showed an awareness of popular news' appeal to a mass audience, and wished, to some extent, to give the people what they wanted. However, this provision of content never matured into an understanding of exactly why mass audiences particularly engaged with popular forms of journalism. Labour's expectations of working-class lives – and their needs and demands – fundamentally clashed with many lived realities of working-class experience in long Edwardian Britain. The result was a 'red' and 'yellow' daily: a popular newspaper that consistently showed disdain towards popular journalism; an everyman's daily that struggled to understand the everyman; a Labour party struggling to appreciate the real lives of the workers they assumed to naturally represent.

For Labour, therefore, the rise of the new popular press evoked the most powerful and complex set of reactions. On the one hand, the new dailies represented the antithesis of how many socialists envisioned the press. Far from being a watchdog or part of the fourth estate, the new dailies sold news on scandal, sensation and sport on pages surrounded by dominant voices from advertising and business interests. Not only did these key features of the papers appal traditional socialist attitudes towards journalistic responsibility and the influence of capital, but they were (more so than any prior generation of newspaper) a direct threat to the socialist cause. Their cheap prices and focus on 'soft' news made them a direct rival as educator of the mass, lower-paid and lower-educated British public. Labour understood both themselves and the newspaper press as educators of the people, and by teaching them the wrong kinds of lessons, the new dailies were a menace that opposed much of what the party and movement believed most strongly.

However, this burning mistrust and borderline hatred existed alongside a belief that these newspapers offered Labour unprecedented access to the mass audiences of 'men in the street' to whom they longed to spread their own political messages. However, rather than communicating with these newspapers, Labour decided to launch a popular daily of their own. The resulting publication – the *Daily Citizen* – was an uncomfortable union of traditional mistrust and newfound opportunity. Its pages would simultaneously try to emulate the new daily formula, while attacking the very press they were demonstrably copying at the same time. This clash became so fraught that one column devoted to New Journalism human interest would be alongside articles mocking the content of other New Journalism-inspired popular dailies.

This short-lived experiment combining media populism with political purpose was how Labour saw out the Long Edwardian period. As Beers has argued, it would take until almost a decade after the Armistices before Labour began more-substantially exploring popular media to further its political success.[56] However, Labour was reacting to the popular press's political worth as that press itself was first emerging. During this first cycle however, Labour's appreciation of the opportunity could not overcome long-standing and bitter misgivings over the perceived immorality, virtue and purpose that this new popular press. It was Labour, more so than any other Edwardian political party, that saw the new dailies as a political opportunity; they were just unable to equate their qualities with their own understanding of what a 'political newspaper' should be.

Liberals: Laissez-Faire

Just as Labour were receiving initial contact from supporters pleading the case for a socialist daily newspaper, the party was establishing itself as a significant parliamentary force thanks in some degree to a pact made in 1903 between Ramsey MacDonald and Herbert Gladstone, the youngest son of four-time Liberal Prime Minister William Gladstone. This agreement ensured that twenty-four ultimately successful Labour candidates would campaign against Conservatives in the general election three years later without a third candidate splitting the anti-Tory vote.[57] Labour returned the favour to Gladstone's party by also refusing to stand candidates in election constituencies where their presence may have helped a Conservative win by splitting the vote. In this regard, the two parties shared a similar understanding of the political arena in which they both competed. In matters of the new dailies however, the two parties could hardly have been further apart.

After winning victory in 1906, the long Edwardian period was primarily defined, politically at least, by a succession of Liberal governments. Not only would this be the final time that a British Liberal party would hold a popular or parliamentary majority, but it was a period of political history later defined by key pieces of legislation that sought to benefit Britain's poorer citizens. The governments of Henry Campbell-Bannerman and Herbert Asquith – collectively called hereafter the 'New Liberal' governments – implemented various social and economic reforms that lay the foundations of the welfare state later created by the post-1945 Labour governments under Clement Attlee.

These policies, which included old-age pensions, unemployment support and that were paid for in-part by increased taxations on inherited and landed wealth, were representative of a broader ideological shift within British Liberalism. This shift, perhaps most notably defined by then-Chancellor of the Exchequer David Lloyd George defining the general elections of 1910 as a battle between 'peers' (and their Conservative Unionist allies) and the 'people', overtly placed lower-middle and working-class interests at the heart of Liberal political policy. Moreover, the landslide victory of 1906 was fought primarily around issues of Chinese Labour, the threat this posed to British workers, and the potential cost of Conservative tariff reforms on the average, poorer-paid British citizen. The clarification of the latter issue by some Liberal election propaganda as a choice between a Liberal 'big loaf' and a tariff-caused 'little loaf' further clarified the perception of the Liberal party as, more so than ever before, a party fighting to represent and appeal to the British working- and lower-middle classes.

Considering this unprecedented policy emphasis on the interests of the man in the street, it is tempting as a historian to have expected the New Liberalism to have positively engaged in some way or another with a newly emerged mass press that catered so successfully to large readerships. The reality however, from what remains at those archives visited for this book, was a near-complete absence of surviving reactions to the new dailies from within the Liberal ranks, both before and after their spells in government. Despite reaching millions of primarily lower-middle and working-class people every day, at a time when the voices of the kinds of people regularly purchasing the new dailies had never held more political weight then they did during the Long Edwardian era, the Liberal party, on the face value of the records investigated in this book, were largely disinterested in the rise of the new dailies.

It would be tempting, considering the lack of archived Liberal reactions to the new dailies, to reach far-reaching conclusions about attitudes within Edwardian L/liberalism and their relationship with the British electorate. Considering the dramatic collapse of the party after World War I, where the party's share of the national vote slumped from the mid-forties pre-war to less than eighteen percent in 1924, the party's seeming unwillingness to engage with or react to the political potential of the new dailies does carry some significance. The party's seeming collective failure to acknowledge the rise of this new mass press and its communicative possibilities is a tempting new addition to histories of the Liberal party's post-war decline. It adds to traditional histories of decline primarily concerned with schisms at the party's highest levels both personally (the wartime split between Asquith and Lloyd-George) and ideologically by offering a tantalising glimpse of broader party attitudes through the pre-war period towards popular media and popular political communication. Through their lack of reactions, the Liberal party collectively overlooked new opportunities to try and communicate political messages through these new, hugely successful national newspapers.

Such party attitudes towards popular newspapers were evident, and have previously been chronicled, within the party's elite. Henry Campbell-Bannerman, similarly to his predecessor as party leader Lord Roseberry, was unwilling and uncomfortable engaging with popular newspapers for political purposes. Both leaders rarely engaged with

newspaper owners or tried to cultivate constructive links to new publications, restricting their rare engagements with the press to close
friends or long-standing party or personal allies. Asquith, one of the
forefathers of the 'New Liberalism', was similarly disinterested in engaging with popular newspapers, preferring 'quality journalism to
quantity' in both his personal and political dealings, which was behaviour later linked to a personal snobbery borne out of his elite university education.[58]

Furthermore, the efforts made by David Lloyd George to build relationships with Lord Northcliffe were primarily motivated by, and
started after, the latter's acquisition of *The Times* in 1908. The former's
interest in the political influence of newspapers, therefore, was targeted
more at Northcliffe's traditional newspapers, rather than the popular
newspapers that would come to define his legacy. Lloyd George would
gradually come to see the benefits of a popular daily newspaper as a
medium for supportive political communication; his successful efforts
to purchase the *Daily Chronicle* were motivated by his desire to have
a friendly organ in the popular press. This recognition of the political
potential of the popular press only occurred after World War I. The
preceding two decades of popular newspaper success had seemingly
passed him, and other members of the Liberal party elite, by.

However, glaring the absence of archived Liberal reactions is, this
book does not want to overextend the conclusions that can be drawn
from this lack of evidence. A lack of archived reactions from within the
party's elite, from the non-exhaustive array of archives accessed to
the author, does not necessarily mean that reactions did not occur at
the time. This study therefore qualifies the extent to which its findings
from the Liberal archives can substantially contribute to histories of
the party as a whole, and particularly its post-war decline.

The fragments that did exist within the archives accessed for this
book were all contained with the papers of David Lloyd George at
London's Parliamentary Archives, and comprised of three documents
which related to the new dailies pre-World War I. The first was among
Lloyd George's newspaper collection, which featured cuttings from articles in which he was the story. Among these was a single article from
a new daily: an article in the *Mirror* published in March 1904 about
his meeting with King Edward VII. This profile reported on Lloyd
George as a 'most interesting figure' and 'one of the most genial and
popular of men', who had 'made his Majesty very desirous of meeting
him'.[59] This single cutting, however, was the only occasion when one
of the new dailies featured in his personal archive of press reports.

The second document was a correspondence written one decade after the *Mirror* cutting, between the Liberal M.P. Neil Primrose and

Lord Northcliffe, writing from his offices at *The Times*. The latter's simple declaration to Primrose, himself the son of former Liberal leader Lord Roseberry, that he liked 'both Winston (Churchill) and Lloyd George very much',[60] points towards the constructive relationship that Lloyd George and Northcliffe possessed, particularly into the outbreak of war. The third document – a letter from Northcliffe to Lloyd George – best encapsulated the archival issues encountered in this investigation of Liberal party reactions to the new dailies. Its content, in which Northcliffe suggests that Lloyd George starts to share policy announcements with 'one or two' trusted people within the 'Unionist Press', offers an example of the new dailies' most prominent proprietor sharing a trusting relationship with a prominent Edwardian politician. However, the document does not carry a date. It was written on 31 October, and must have been written sometime after Northcliffe's acquisition of *The Times* in 1908, as it is written from their offices.[61] However, its lack of specificity underlines the broader problems of overstretching limited archival remains for the purpose of historical argument.

Interestingly, this lack of elite reaction to the new dailies was not entirely reflective of what could be termed broader 'L/liberal' political culture during the Long Edwardian period. Their rise and development may not have sparked very much from party leaders which has survived in the archives, but their existence did gradually filter, for example, into the lexicon of newspapers that were supportive of the Liberal party. The most significant reactions to the new dailies materialised in the *Daily News*: the Cadbury-owned popular daily which Labour had tried to purchase in their early attempts to create a supportive popular newspaper. The *News's* first mention of the *Mail* occurred just over a year after the latter's launch, with the former remarking positively on how it had discovered a 'comic' story out of the thirty-day Greco-Turkish war over Ottoman-occupied Crete, which detailed how an unnamed woman, exasperated with the competence of a local battalion, had enlisted herself to 'come to the rescue'.

This first reaction by a prominent Liberal newspaper to the new dailies formed part of a broader pattern across the Long Edwardian period, which represented the new dailies and the *Daily Mail*, in particular, as an unassuming but not unwelcome addition to the British newspaper industry. For instance, much of their place within the content of the *Daily News* was in the form of adverts or recommendations for upcoming editions of, or stories from, the *Mail*. The most striking of these was a full front-page of the *News* in March 1906 advertising 'The Invasion of 1910': a speculative historical fiction exploring a future invasion of the British Isles featuring a map charting the routes through the which an unnamed invading force had infiltrated Britain.[62] This striking full-page advert for the *Mail*'s 'intensely interesting narrative', seen particularly within the broader context of article recommendations, clearly identified new daily newspapers as publications of interest to readers of this prominent Liberal daily.

The nature of this interest, however, was particular. The occasions when newspapers such as the *Daily News* would refer to one of the three new dailies – of the three it was the *Mail* that was referred to most frequently – in a positive way was in reference to distinctly 'human interest' pieces of content. 'The Invasion of 1910', for example, was an advert for a high-profile piece of fiction, which tapped into a broader cultural fixation on 'invasion narratives' that existed in Britain in the years that would ultimately precede the outbreak of World War I.[63] The place of new dailies within Liberal newspaper discourse, when positive, concerned their ability to entertain, humour or titillate. In contrast to Labour dismissals of this 'feather-brained' content, the Liberal press found positives in the new dailies' more light-hearted approach to daily journalism.

However, when referencing their political content, specifically their election-time political content, the Liberal press's reactions towards the new dailies turned distinctly negative. The new dailies' political value was harshly criticised or openly mocked, and particularly targeted their apparently loose use of supportive evidence. The difference in tone between the endorsements and the criticisms was striking, particularly considering how close together in time these wildly different representations of the new dailies were printed. For example, less than two months before publishing the full-page advert for 'Invasion', the *Daily News* headlined a piece detailing an example of the *Daily Mail's* election coverage as 'A Disgrace to Journalism'. This 'abuse' of reporting standards concerned a quote the *Mail* misattributed to Henry Campbell-Bannerman concerning the issue of 'Chinese slavery': the controversial election issue which had particularly sparked debates over 'pictorial lies' in politics discussed in Chapters 2 and 3. Their coverage was accused of being a 'disgraceful invention' and the type of behaviour which 'degrades an honourable profession'. The piece concluded with a reminder that the man behind this coverage – Lord Northcliffe – had been given an honour by the previous Conservative government, and it strongly suggested this 'disgrace' was an example of political *quid pro quo*;

Perhaps such services (the article which attributed false words to the Liberal leader) *deserve such rewards.*[64]

While the *Mail* was not covered again, either positively or negatively, by the *News* during the 1906 election, this standalone article was hugely significant. It marked a distinct difference in Liberal reaction to the new daily press when considering them as a source of political news, rather than as a medium of entertainment. Where humour and fiction were praised or publicised, election content was viciously and exclusively identified as negative. They were accused of being dishonest in their coverage of the party; their respect for their broader profession brought into question; and their content connected to potential ideological collusion between the paper's owner and their Unionist foe. The Lib-Lab agreement in 1906, it would seem, also appeared to share the same negative opinions of the political new dailies. In contrast to Labour, however, the Liberal party saw only the negative, rather than any communicative positive.

This Liberal hostility towards the politics of the new dailies persisted into the elections of 1910, as the same Liberal-allied newspapers, especially the popular *News* which had hounded the *Mails* 'disgrace' to the profession continued to represent them as wholly negative publications. This negativity had changed from the righteous fury directed at the paper's politics in 1906. In place of fury, the L/Liberal daily press mocked the new dailies, with the *Daily Mail* once again being the primary target of negative coverage. Key to this mockery were persistent references made across several articles to the *Mail* and the factual consistency of its coverage.

One way in which the *Mail* was represented as a comically untrustworthy publication came through the selective printing of political speeches from the election campaign which mentioned the newspaper by name. For example, a section from a David Lloyd-George speech (printed on 10 January 1910) concludes with a slight at the *Mail's* value. After a remark to the crowd asking whether German citizens would be happy eating bad food if good food was available, which was part of a broader argument against proposed Unionist tariffs reforms, he cries;

> *Oh yes, they would. (Laughter). The 'Daily Mail', says they* (German citizens) *like it. (Loud laughter). The 'Daily Mail' says it is wholesome, and the 'Daily Mail' always tells the truth. (Renewed laughter).*[65]

To Lloyd-George and to the crowd, the *Mail* was a punchline. More interestingly, it was a newspaper with a negative identity distinct enough, at least within Liberal political culture of the election, to make the joke both obvious and, considering the included crowd response, well-received. Indeed, it was a joke echoed across other parts of the *News's* election coverage. The paper's daily *Table Talk* column began one day's summaries with an almost-identical comment on the *Mail's* untruthful reputation, summarising its leading articles during the December election of 1910 as entities that "can usually be depended upon, in any crisis, for the best display of earnest fatuity".[66] Moreover, these jokes were attacks against the *Mail* as a whole, rather than specifically its political coverage. While its politics was still targeted by the *News* as it had been in 1906, this broader mockery of the *Mail's* value as a newspaper represented a hardening of L/Liberal towards its broader journalistic value. It was a publication to laugh at; defined by its empty-headed thoughts and lack of basic, competent accuracy. The inclusion of full-page adverts for the *Mail's* content were now distinctly part of the L/Liberal press's past.

Another speech, delivered by MP Walter Runciman and selected for print in the *Daily News,* attacked the *Mail's* place in British culture, promising that a Liberal government (if returned) would not consider the comment of the *Mail* in its formation of policy, and that "the value of the *Daily Mail* articles might be judged by the proved inaccuracy of the only figures they contained".[67] The latter point carried similar sentiments to the Lloyd-George joke, by critically summarising the real-world value of the *Mail* by its supposed habit of inaccurate news reporting. It was however, tinged with less joviality than the crowd-loved gag of days before. In this case, it reads more as a bitter quip; a joke that mocks, but with a resentful appreciation of the significance of that which it mocks. In this case, the 'inaccuracy'-laced *Mail* was a newspaper which, up to that point, held sway in British culture. Runciman accused the paper and some of its writers of holding undue and considerable influence over current policy. Similar to the 1906 tirade against the paper's conduct, this L/Liberal representation of the new dailies echoed sentiments within Labour. However, while sharing an appreciation of the power that such a press's political significance had, L/Liberalism again stopped short of Labour's reactions; they saw the significance, but not what they could do to potentially incorporate it into their own political strategies.

The earlier ignorance of the Liberal party elite, therefore, was not entirely indicative of a broader party ignorance of popular newspapers and their potential political and cultural significance. First enthusiastically and later begrudgingly, voices within the Liberal-supportive press indicated an appreciation of the significant place which the new dailies and the *Daily Mail*, in particular, held in the wider culture of Long Edwardian Britain. Their human-interest content was referenced with encouragement to readers of L/Liberal newspapers throughout the first portion of the period; it was news that was thought to be of interest to readers who, come an election, were likelier than not to vote for a Liberal candidate. Even when representing newspapers such as the *Mail* in a negative manner, as became more pronounced during and after the landslide election victory of 1906, there was the idea that these new popular newspapers had a wider significance. While politically unpalatable to Liberal politicians and commentators, the new dailies were a phenomena worthy of consideration.

Much of this consideration, however, was negative, and the ways in which British L/liberalism either ignored or mocked the political potential of the new dailies was distinct and ubiquitous. While kinder words were found for elements of their non-political coverage, the new dailies' contribution to British political culture was never positive from a L/liberal perspective. The negativity expressed towards them was characterised mainly as mockery: comic disdain that echoed the 'feather-brained' origins of the new dailies' forebears. This mockery however, coupled with more isolated barbed attacks against the integrity and the supposed influence of the *Mail* on Unionist policy, was suggestive of a broader appreciation within Long Edwardian L/liberalism of the political power, however objectionable, of the new dailies by the end of the period. The mockery was not of a press without influence; the jokes against its character, and jokes that were not levelled against other pro-Unionist newspapers during either 1906 or 1910, spoke of its particular place within L/Liberal election-time press discourse. This appreciation was gradual in growth and not reflected by the party elite, but it did exist.

This broader L/liberal press discourse concerning the politics of the new dailies did, however, contain further evidence that spoke of the broader ignorance or disdain towards the new dailies from the party's elite, from what has remained within the selected archives. The speeches printed that mocked the *Mail* were from significant party figures, including the then-Chancellor and future party leader Lloyd-George. Their possible private disinterest in the new dailies was supported by public-facing disinterest in the form of quoted mockery. Rather than being a closed secret, powerful voices within the Liberal elite were comfortable expressing their disinterest in engaging with the new dailies on the campaign trail. This was in interesting contrast to Labour, where broader hostility to the new dailies in public was contrasted by intense inner-party plans to try and use them as inspiration for their own political purposes. The Long Edwardian Liberals, in this sense, went further in their critical dismissal of the new dailies than the more publicly hostile Labour movement.

One of the reasons behind both the initial ignorance and the later, more-complete new daily hostility from the Liberals likely lay in the fact that British L/Liberalism, contrast to Labour, already had a significant daily newspaper presence in the form of the dailies *News* and *Chronicle*. While Labour saw new daily success as a lesson to translate to their own ends, the Liberals understood only a political and journalistic competitor. The new dailies were not a political or journalistic inspiration; they were a political and journalistic irritant unworthy of more than mocking resentment.

This resentment however also spoke of an undeniable ignorance or unwillingness within the party and its press allies to draw inspiration from its unprecedented success. Labour was just as hostile, if not more so, to the new dailies' supposed impact on political and press culture, but also saw, however crudely, how their particular approach to journalism could be appropriated for their own political ends. The Liberals, by contrast, never reacted to the new dailies with any real serious consideration of their possible merits. This was not entirely explained by the prior existence of a pro-Liberal press. Labour too, had multiple, if admittedly less prominent, supportive publications that did not hinder the party's ability to appreciate the communicative potential of this new daily popular press. Instead, this Liberal ignorance tied back to the unwillingness of the party's elite to engage with this new press through anything more than occasionally quoted jokes. Their comfort with the supportive press they had was in stark contrast to Labour's mind-set, and spoke of a broader inability to see the new dailies as anything but either a 'human interest' daily or a pro-Unionist organ, thus an entity unworthy of serious consideration.

While just as much an 'enemy' to their politics as they were to Labour, the Liberals' limited reactions to the new dailies, from their private silence to their public quips, do suggest a difference between the two parties understanding of the popular press and its potential for speaking to a mass public. The Long Edwardian Liberals were content with the press support they already had, and were disinterested in the potential of the new dailies as they failed to see it beyond simple partisan lines. The sparse nature of archived reactions, however, does temper the extent of the conclusions regarding broader Liberal attitudes to the rise of the new dailies during the Long Edwardian period.

Conservatives: Office Boys

While they differed fundamentally in their appreciation of the potential of the new dailies' political content, the Liberals and Labour shared one core belief about this emergent press: that it was antagonistic to their respective political ideologies, particularly during general elections. There was little doubt that all three of the new dailies were broadly supportive of the Conservative Unionists throughout all four general elections of the Long Edwardian period. The regularity with which both Liberal and Labour commentators lamented or mocked the pro-Unionist politics of these new newspapers would suggest, to the modern historian, that the party and this new press were actively cooperating in some form or another. Indeed, as the previous section discussed, accusations of collusion between the new dailies and governing Unionists were sometimes made explicit. The level of 'collusion', in reality, was far less than those occasional conspiratorial voices implied. Indeed, for much of the Long Edwardian period, the political significance new dailies were of as little consequence to Unionist party as they were for the Liberals. There were, however, noticeable exceptions to this ignorance.

At the beginning of this period, the Conservatives were the newly dominant party in British politics. Under Lord Salisbury, the Conservatives (and their Liberal Unionist allies)[68] had won a huge majority at the general election of 1895, returning 234 more MPs than Lord Rosebery's defeated Liberals.[69] They would hold office until the landslide defeat of 1906 and would win another huge parliamentary majority in the 'khaki' general election of 1900. As such, they governed during the period between 1896 and 1903 during which all three of the new daily popular newspapers launched.

Current historical knowledge into the Conservative's reactions to the new popular press is framed around interactions between leading party members and the editors and proprietors of newspapers. These existing understandings of individual Conservative politician's relationships with the new popular dailies will be re-examined by drawing out these examples of interpersonal relationships as evidence of underlying attitudes to the new popular press as a whole. After re-exploring these relationships, material from both personal and party-wide archives will further explore the broader reactions of agents across the party towards the emerging popular daily press.

Stephen Koss's chapter looking into the relationships between prominent Unionist MP Joseph Chamberlain and the proprietors of the three new dailies broadly structures their discourse as a long-running series of calculated power plays between the three individuals. Chamberlain is cast in the role of press orchestrator, while the two proprietors are portrayed as powerful, competing personalities from whom Chamberlain sought both public political backing and personal rivalry for his attention.[70]

This interpretation of their interactions places the single politician at its heart, with the two proprietors being just part of a wider 'crowd' reacting and responding to the whims and actions of this lead actor and his supporters, who themselves are mere extensions of the lead personality through their title of 'Chamberlainites'.[71] These same interactions provide initial insight into the wider reactions across the Conservative party to the rise of the new daily popular press. This is because, rather than being standalone interactions, Chamberlain's dialogues infer attitudes towards the new dailies that were shared by many across his party. His access to their proprietors was relatively unique, but his underlying attitude towards their newspapers was not.

Joseph Chamberlain's encounters with the proprietors of the *Mail, Express* and *Mirror,* as previously identified by Koss, show a proactive move by the politician to use these newspapers to disseminate and even actively support his primary policy objectives. Chamberlain wanted to use these popular newspapers to publicize his push for Imperial protection: a tariff on internationally imported goods which benefitted domestic and dominion traders by raising the price of materials brought in from outside British-controlled territories. This single proposed piece of legislation became Chamberlain's primary, all-consuming political objective, to such an extent that he was campaigning separately both from the staunchly free-trade Liberals and the leader of his own party, A. J. Balfour from 1903 until the calamitous general election defeat in 1906.[72]

According to Koss's analysis, Chamberlains 'use' of the *Mail* and the *Express* was part of a broader history of political actors in Britain liaising with the press to further their own political aims. In one sense this is correct; the rise of the new dailies did not provoke an original response from leading Conservative politicians as to how to communicate with them. The ways in which Chamberlain liaised with this new press did not deviate significantly from how past generations of leading Conservatives had reacted to a press. The new dailies, to some extent, added to a longer tradition of newspapers that could be spoken with in order to communicate Conservative messages to wider audiences.

What was relatively unique about elite Conservative reactions to these new popular daily newspapers was the rationale behind their interest in these particular titles. To refer again to Chamberlain, his particularly keen interest in developing relationships with Harmsworth and Pearson was motivated by the uniquely popular appeal of their new newspapers. For example, his initial scepticism in building bridges with Pearson because of the latter's assumed attitude towards imperial protection was overridden specifically because of the large readerships that the *Express* had been able to rapidly gain since its launch.[73] Similarly with Harmsworth, concerns about personal differences were inferior to the mass appeal of their newspapers, and the large reach that their titles had in terms of mass popular readerships was the fundamental motivation behind Chamberlain's targeting of their favour and interest.

This marks out the new dailies as distinct from their contemporaries, as their uniquely large readerships were the principal factor motivating the nature of Chamberlain's reactions to them. Whereas the longer history of Conservative elites saw them court relationships with a host of editors and proprietors, Chamberlain deliberately focused attention primarily on the owners of the *Daily Mail* and the *Daily Express*. The reaction to this new press was directly informed by their singular popular appeal and large daily readerships. By principally focusing on just these two proprietors during his years of attempting to further his campaign for imperial protection, Chamberlain's reactions to the new dailies spoke of the unique opportunity these newspapers provided for speaking to mass audiences of people; audiences that previous generations of politicians would have needed the assistance of dozens of newspapers to potentially communicate with.

Broader *Gleanings*

Among the surviving party records explored in this book, Chamberlain stood mostly alone in seeing the new dailies as an exciting new opportunity, and his tariff-campaigning enthusiasm for their communicative potential stood out as an exception, who responded to this new press by seeing its far-reaching political possibilities. Perhaps, to refer back to Chapter 1, Lord Salisbury's 'office boys' dismissal rang true across broader swathes of the Conservative party elite.

When broadening out to consider the place of the new dailies in the eyes and minds of less elite party activists however, the popular press's significance in Edwardian C/conservative political life is more nuanced. In contrast to leading political figures, there lacks sufficient private records of more junior party activists to allow for an accurate insight into wider reactions. However, the early Conservative party archives do contain a set of records that allows historians a degree of access into how the new popular press was understood and reacted to by the rank and file members of the Conservative party: *National Union Gleanings*.[74]

Beginning in 1893, *National Union Gleanings* (and its successor from 1912 onwards, *Gleanings and Memoranda*) was a monthly journal of record, created and published by the Conservative Party. It was created for, and circulated to, agents at all levels of the Conservative Party: MPs, agents and speakers. Its primary intention was as a notebook for Conservative activists, providing basic information on a variety of political subjects from a wide array of source materials. These source materials included minutes from internal meetings, reports from rallies of both Conservative and opposition MPs, memos and notes passed around Parliament, and extracts from a wide selection of newspapers. The inclusion of the new dailies in these monthly party notebooks sheds considerable insight into not only how the new dailies were being seen across virtually all levels of the party, but how these newspapers were understood by party elites who ran and distributed *Gleanings* to party members.

Since *Gleanings* began publication, newspaper cuttings were used to give readers details of political events both at home and abroad. These cuttings commonly came with an attached recommendation to read the longer article from which the included section was repurposed. At the time that the first of the dailies emerged, the most prominent newspapers cited by *Gleanings* were *The Times*, the *Daily News* and the *Daily Chronicle*. The latter two were included primarily when giving the Liberal view of an event, as both newspapers had strong ties to the Liberal party and were the most prominent non-Conservative newspapers in Late-Victorian Britain. *The Times* meanwhile, consistently the most cited individual newspaper in each monthly edition of *Gleanings,* was a frequent reference point for Conservative news, usually incorporating much of the same kinds of material sought from the *News* and the *Chronicle*, with the addition of a frequent inclusion of letters to the editor. While certainly the most prominent individual newspaper sources, the journal also include cuttings from publications across the country, ranging from magazines such as the prominent *Fortnightly Review* to local newspapers such as the *Western Morning News*.[75]

It was into this *Gleanings* tradition of newspaper cuttings that the *Daily Mail* and later *Daily Express* slowly established themselves.[76] Even though the *Daily Mail* launched to almost instant popular success[77] it did not become part *Gleaning's* repertoire of newspaper sources until the March issue of 1897. This first utterance of the *Daily Mail* was because of an article it published which contained a declaration by a 'high ranking' native official in the Transvaal (a neighbouring state to British-controlled South Africa) regarding the strong and insurmountable 'race hatred' between the occupying British and the Boers.[78] In the same issue of *Gleanings,* the *Mail* is included again for its coverage of issues in the Transvaal. In this instance, it references an article which offers a step-by-step breakdown of a phrase used by President Kruger (then president of the South African Republic) to describe Queen Victoria. The words used – 'een kwaje vrouw' – are broken down to explore their insulting meaning to readers, through reference to English equivalents; 'kwaje' is linked to the British word 'queer' (meaning odd), although it is stressed that the Boer's version of the word is far greater in "wickedness".[79]

The ways in which the *Daily Mail* is first used in *National Union Gleanings* were broadly twofold. On the one hand, its inclusion is for its coverage of imperial matters, and specifically for its coverage of anti-British controversies. On the other, the specific nature of the articles chosen for inclusion within *Gleanings* constructed the *Mail* as a newspaper to provide summaries of a complex topic. In the first article, the paper's emphasis on dramatic race-specific language creates the tensions surrounding the Transvaal as ones of binary racial divides: Boer versus Brit. In the second, its inclusion is for the purposes of topic simplification. It provided a plainly described, step-by-step guide through the offending phrase, and why exactly it was offensive to the Queen.

The *Daily Mail* would continue to appear in *Gleanings* after this point, but only rarely. Its next use after its debut would be exactly one year later, and would, again, be for its particular coverage of imperial matters. In one instance, it is included to, again, detail behaviour in the Transvaal that is confrontational to the British, with its summary of Boer seizures of British-owned mining lands.[80] In the other, its summarising of the 1898 Local Government (Ireland) Bill is included under the heading 'The Scheme Explained'.[81] After a full year of not being included, the *Mail* was again used in *Gleanings* in a specific way which represented it as a newspaper that provided concise, easy to understand information about political topics, and was particularly invested in colonial issues.

This pattern of inclusion in *Gleanings* would continue both for the *Daily Mail* and, after 1900, the *Daily Express.* Similar to the *Mail,* the Express had to wait for over a year of circulation[82] before entering *Gleanings* as a source of relevant and useful information for Conservative agents. When seen together, the new dailies became used for very similar reasons as the *Mail* had been since it was first introduced into the journal. The two papers were included primarily when discussing imperial matters, and more specifically the troubles in South Africa and the Second Boer War. Indeed, the first inclusion of the *Express* is very similar to that of the *Mail,* as it is an article lamenting how dying Boer children seemed to illicit more sympathy from politicians than the deaths of British women and children in the same region.[83] The similarity here comes both in the provocative nature of the included piece, similar to the 'race hate' debut of the *Mail,* and the simplicity of what the piece has to say.

The inclusions of both the *Mail* and the *Express* in *Gleanings* would continue to follow the general themes seen in their earliest inclusions. Over time, the topic of the chosen cuttings would diversify from solely pro-imperial or colonial matters. For example, both papers were included side by side in a section detailing the emigration of military workmen from Woolwich Arsenal to Germany,[84] and sections from both papers were used within a month of each other to outline some of the policies of,[85] and need for resistance against,[86] British socialism. However, colonial and international coverage from these two papers still featured strongly, such as the *Express's* discussion regarding the employment of non-British workers in the navy.[87]

What is striking when looking at how these two new popular dailies were included in this Conservative party journal is how specifically the papers were utilised. It is important to point out that the topics that both the *Mail* and the *Express* were used to discuss were not unique to them. Other newspapers and magazines included in *Gleanings* discussed the same political topics seen in the cuttings of the new dailies; the empire, socialism and industry. Also, neither of the dailies were unique in how they discussed these issues in terms of emotive language; the frequent inclusion of speeches and editorials from elsewhere carried similar levels of emotive, partisan political standpoints as were used in the new dailies. Moreover, the *Mail* and the *Express* were not the only newspapers who were used to offer simplified versions of political news. Almost every publication included in *Gleanings,* from *The Times* to *Reynolds Newspaper,* was used at point or another to give a concise summary of a broader topic or particular complex issue.

What made the new dailies unique, however, was how this emphasis on short simplicity, clarity of expression and passionate, partisan language was present in the vast majority of inclusions. Whereas other newspapers, such as *The Times*, the *Daily News* or the *Daily Chronicle*, would occasionally talk about the same topics in the same kinds of language, this was not their sole focus. The inclusions of the new dailies were, in comparison to other more traditional national newspapers and magazines of the period, few and far between, with use of their content separated by several months or sometimes over a year. Then, on the few occasions they were included in *Gleanings*, it was using sections of articles that, regardless of the story, were framed as summaries, break-downs or step-by-step, hand-holding explanations of topics. Their inclusions were headlined by *Gleanings* with words like 'summary', 'guide', or 'what does it mean?'. Their cuttings were often no more than a paragraph or two,[88] and sometimes certain phrases or words were highlighted in bold by the makers of *Gleanings*,[89] likely to point readers towards key words within already short inclusions.

The ways in which *National Union Gleanings* incorporated the new dailies *Mail* and *Express* shed interesting light on how they may have been seen and understand by the wider Conservative party in Long Edwardian Britain. Within this grassroots party publication, the new dailies were represented as newspapers defined by simplicity of expression and use of plain, often blunt, language. Their extremely irregular inclusion in these monthly journals showcased them as newspapers best read for stripped down summaries and emotional, accessible descriptions of politics that had a strong pro-imperial, anti-Radical, and anti-socialist ideology. They did not become a regular or prominent source of news like *The Times* or the traditional Liberal dailies, but became occasional, brief, and simplistic contributors to the informing of the wider party. For all of their incredible popular success, and for all the attention paid to their owners by limited elite sections of the party, the wider Conservative party was reacting to the new popular press in ways which suggested a level of interest an enthusiasm for its content different from both much of the mass public and their own party leaders and elites. While not dismissed out of hand, their vibrant place at the heart of British news culture was not reflected in their place within grassroots Conservative party culture. Far from being integral allies of the party – as voices within Edwardian Labour and the Liberals accused – the new dailies occupied a minor place within the wider Conservative party and its relationship with the newspaper industry of the period.

That is, until the very end of the Long Edwardian era, when the Conservatives created a new official party post. This post was first held by John Malcolm Fraser, who would later receive a knighthood for his wartime services to the Admiralty. Before these military heroics, however, he was appointed to a new role: Advisor to the Conservative Party on Press Matters. Before this new appointment, he was a writer and journalist: among of those past roles was an editorial role at the *Daily Express*. Frustratingly, almost nothing has survived in the archive which documents his years in this position pre-1914. However, the very notion of his hiring – a former editor of a new daily newspaper, tasked with liaising with the press on behalf of the Conservative Party – points tantalisingly at a growing awareness at the political significance of the new dailies.

This awareness can also be seen within a letter sent in 1912 from then-leader Andrew Bonar Law's surviving correspondence with Ralph David Blumenfeld: editor of the *Daily Express* between 1902 and 1932, and previously a news editor at the *Daily Mail* from 1900. Their only other surviving previous correspondence, sent two years earlier, had seen the former reject the latter's request for information regarding an upcoming article saying that he 'really cannot possibly find time to do what you suggest'.[90] Two years after that refusal, Bonar Law wrote to the editor of the *Express* requesting that one of his writers, a 'Mr. Pollock', send a copy of a forthcoming article to 'Mr. Thornton'.[91] The significance of this comes from the fact that Mr Thornton with whom Bonar Law wanted the *Express* to liaise was, at the time of the letter, the private secretary to Arthur Steel-Maitland: the Conservative Party Chairman from 1911 to 1916.

Bonar Law's willingness to engage with *Express* by the end of the Long Edwardian period, which occurred after the hiring of Fraser as a press advisor, was also noted by the owners of the new dailies. In a letter noted by the archivist to have been written between December 1911 and January 1913, Lord Northcliffe wrote to Max Aitken, the later Lord Beaverbrook and then significant investor in the *Daily Express* about a possible future meeting that suggested that the hiring of Fraser had reaped some direct contact with the new dailies;

> *I wired today suggesting that Bonar Law might be able to come to Sutton* (Northcliffe's private residence) *on Sunday and talk shop and play golf.*[92]

While the response to this proposed meeting was not among the fragments of the current archive, the fact that the owner of the *Daily Mail* and the *Daily Mirror* was writing to the future owner of the *Daily Express* with the belief that he could invite the current Conservative leader (and a future Prime Minister) to his private residence to play golf together and 'talk shop' shows a significant development across the Long Edwardian period. Not only had the new dailies grown into becoming significant forces within the British press and political culture of the period, but the leader of the Conservative party, by the end of the period, was moving within the same social circle. The likelihood of Lord Salisbury socialising and talking 'shop' with the proprietors of a newspaper which he saw fit only for 'office boys' underlines the development across the period within the Conservative party, which saw the significance of the new dailies develop.

Notes

1 Aspects of the following two sub-sections have been accepted for future publication. See Christopher Shoop-Worrall, 'The *Daily Citizen:* Class v Consumerism in the Early Labour Press' in 9780367361341 | *Routledge History of the Working Class in the West* | Edn. 1 | Hardback Origin UK | Chapter.
2 Letters from G. Stephenson to R. J. MacDonald, 15 February–20 March 1904, sourced at People's History Museum, Manchester. Accessed April 2016.
3 Regrettably, the author's name is unclear from his signature or return postal address. Closest reading suggested it may have been 'Frank Kennedy'.
4 Letters to R. J. Macdonald, 29 January 1906, sourced at People's History Museum, Manchester. Accessed April 2016.
5 'The Need of a Daily', *Labour Leader* 27 September 1907.
6 'The Daily Mail Dodge', *Labour Leader* 1 March 1907.
7 'The Modern Daily Press', *The Cooperative News* 5 January 1907.
8 For more on the transatlantic histories of the popular press, see Wiener, *The Americanization of the British Press, 1830s-1914 : Speed in the Age of Transatlantic Journalism.*
9 'The Indian Press', *Labour Leader* 22 February 1907.
10 See Joan Allen and Owen R. Ashton, *Papers for the People : A Study of the Chartist Press* (London: Merlin Press, 2005); George Boyce, James Curran, and Pauline Wingate, *Newspaper History from the Seventeenth Century to the Present Day* (Published for the Press Group of the Acton Society [by] Constable, 1978), 62; James Epstein, 'Feargus O'Connor and the Northern Star', *International Review of Social History* 21, no. 1 (18 April 1976): 51–97, https://doi.org/10.1017/S0020859000005137; James Epstein, *The Lion of Freedom : Feargus O'Connor and the Chartist Movement, 1832-1842* (London: Croom Helm, 1982); Patricia Hollis, *The Pauper Press : A Study in Working-Class Radicalism of the 1830s* (Oxford: Oxford University Press, 1970); Paul A. Pickering, *Feargus O'Connor : A Political Life* (London: Merlin Press, 2008); Joel H. Wiener, *The War of*

the Unstamped : The Movement to Repeal the British Newspaper Tax, 1830-1836 (Ithaca, NY: Cornell University Press, 1969).

11 See Martin Hewitt, *The Dawn of the Cheap Press in Victorian Britain: The End of the 'Taxes on Knowledge', 1849–1869* (London: Bloomsbury, 2014); Jonathan Samples, 'Working-Class Prose: The "Northern Star" and Radical Discourse during the First-Wave of the Chartist Movement – ProQuest' (MA Thesis: Roosevelt University, 2013).

12 'Should Football be Stopped?: Its Effect upon the Public Mind and the Country's Crisis', *The Cooperative News*, 21 November 1914.

13 "Drink and Legislation" and "Drinking Clubs", *Labour Leader* 6 March 1908.

14 'A Challenge for Socialism: The Express Man Spoiling for a Fight', *Labour Leader*, 10 January 1908; 'The Challenge for Socialism: The Express's Frigid Reply', *Labour Leader* 17 January 1908.

15 Letters from G. Stephenson to R. J. MacDonald, 15 February–20 March 1904, sourced at People's History Museum, Manchester. Accessed April 2016.

16 Letters to R. J. Macdonald, 21 January–29 January 1906, sourced at People's History Museum, Manchester. Accessed April 2016.

17 'The Need of a Daily', *Labour Leader* 27 September 1907.

18 'A New Socialist Daily', *Labour Leader* 20 September 1907.

19 Brown, *First Labour Party*, pp. 113–24.

20 Resolution No. XXXIII 'Plea for a Labour Paper', *The Trades Union Congress Parliamentary Committee*, October 1903.

21 In response to the TUC, the party initially issued a newsletter to 'the Trade Unions of the United Kingdom' with side-by-side lists of the issues and merits of a daily versus a weekly paper, with the weekly coming out as clear winner (7 May 1904).

22 Ramsay MacDonald, *Memorandum RE Labour Newspaper*, 10 December 1903.

23 Deian Hopkins, 'The Socialist Press in Britain, 1890-1910', in *Newspaper History from the Seventeenth Century to the Present Day*, ed. James Curran, George Boyce, and Pauline Wingate (London: Sage/Constable, 1978), 265–80.

24 Carolyn Malone, 'Campaigning Journalism: The Clarion, the Daily Citizen, and the Protection of Women Workers, 1898-1912', *Labour History Review* 67, no. 3 (2002): 281–97.

25 Stanley Harrison, *Poor Men's Guardians : A Record of the Struggles for a Democratic Newspaper Press, 1763-1973* (London: Lawrence and Wishart, 1974), 174–75.

26 Rachael Claire Attwood, 'Vice beyond the Pale: Representing "White Slavery" in Britain, c.1880 - 1912', (Doctoral Thesis: UCL, University College London, 2013).

27 'Young Girls in Peril', *Daily Citizen* 1 January 1913, p. 3.

28 'White Slave Traps', *Daily Citizen* 4 January 1913, p. 8.

29 'White Slavers at Work', *Daily Citizen* 18 January 1913, p. 1.

30 'Mrs Churchill in Motor Smash', *Daily Citizen* 20 January 1913, p. 3.

31 *Daily Citizen* 27 June 1913, p. 1.

32 'Woman Worked to Death', *Daily Citizen* 1 January 1913, p. 1.

33 *Daily Citizen* 23 May 1913, p. 1.

34 Boyle and Haynes, *Power Play: Sport, the Media and Popular Culture*, 19–42.
35 Holt, *Sport and the British: A Modern History*, 306–7.
36 Brown, *Victorian News and Newspapers*, 271–72.
37 Jan Chovanec, '"...But There Were No Broken Legs"', *Journal of Historical Pragmatics* 15, no. 2 (2014): 228–54, https://doi.org/10.1075/jhp.15.2.05cho.
38 *Daily Citizen* 19 April 1913.
39 'A Thrilling Cup Final', *Daily Citizen* 21 April 1913, p. 8.
40 Ibid., p. 3.
41 *Daily Citizen* 2 January 1913.
42 Ibid., 3 May 1913.
43 Ibid., 19 April 1913.
44 *Daily Citizen* 3 May 1913.
45 Ibid.
46 Bingham and Conboy, *Tabloid Century*, p. 6.
47 *Daily Citizen* 10 January 1913, p. 6.
48 Ibid., 21 January 1913, p. 6.
49 Ibid., 7 January 1913, p. 4.
50 'Should Football be Stopped?', *Cooperative News* 21 November 1914.
51 *Daily Citizen* 20 January 1913, p. 7.
52 'Their Views and Ours', *Daily Citizen* 9 June 1913, p. 2.
53 Ibid., 27 June 1913.
54 Ibid., 1 July 1913.
55 Ibid., 3 May 1913.
56 Laura Beers, *Your Britain: Media and the Making of the Labour Party* (Cambridge, MA: Harvard University Press, 2010), 116–38.
57 Martin Pugh, *The Making of Modern British Politics, 1867-1945* (London: Blackwells, 2002), 117.
58 J. M. McEwen, 'Lloyd George's Acquisition of the Daily Chronicle in 1918', *Journal of British Studies* 22, no. 1 (1982): 127–44, https://doi.org/10.2307/175660.
59 'Mr Lloyd George Meets His Majesty', *Daily Mirror* 12 March 1904, Lloyd George papers, Parliamentary Archives [LG/A/12/1/29].
60 Letter from Lord Northcliffe to Neil Primrose M.P. 17 March 1914, Lloyd George papers, Parliamentary Archives [LG/C/11/1/1].
61 Letter from Lord Northcliffe to David Lloyd George, 31 October (post-1908), Lloyd George papers, Parliamentary Archives [LG/C/6/8/1].
62 'The Invasion of 1910', *Daily News* 13 March 1906, p. 1.
63 Michael Hughes and Harry Wood, 'Crimson Nightmares: Tales of Invasion and Fears of Revolution in Early Twentieth-Century Britain', *Contemporary British History* 28, no. 3 (3 July 2014): 294–317, https://doi.org/10.1080/13619462.2014.941817.
64 'A Disgrace to Journalism', *Daily News* 11 January 1906, p. 6.
65 'The Speech', *Daily News* 10 January 1910, p. 6.
66 'Table Talk', *Daily News* 14 December 1910, p. 6.
67 'Mr Runciman, M.P.', *Daily News* 20 January 1910, p. 4.
68 For much of this period, the Conservatives were named the 'Unionists' to account for the combining of the original party and the Liberal defectors. Throughout this study, the two names for the party will be used interchangeably to refer to the same, broader collective.

69 Paul Readman, 'The 1895 General Election and Political Change in Late Victorian Britain', *The Historical Journal* 42, no. 2 (1999): 467–93.

70 Koss, *The Rise and Fall of the Political Press in Britain, Volume II*, 15–53.

71 Ibid., 36.

72 Peter Marsh, *Joseph Chamberlain: Entrepreneur in Politics* (New Haven, CT: Yale University Press, 1994), 581–631.

73 Ibid.

74 All references to *National Union Gleanings* come from research at the Bodleian Library. Special thanks is owed to Jeremy McIlwaine, Conservative Party Archivist at Oxford's Weston Library for highlighting this material.

75 *National Union Gleanings,* January 1901, Index

76 The *Daily Mirror* does not feature in *Gleanings.*

77 Dennis Griffiths, *Fleet Street : Five Hundred Years of the Press* (London: British Library, 2006), 132–33.

78 'Daily Mail, Feb. 4th 1897', *National Union Gleanings*, 'Provocative Boer Utterance', March 1897.

79 'Daily Mail, March 16th 1897', *National Union Gleanings*, 'What Does It Mean?', March 1897.

80 'The *Daily Mail* on Boer Cupidity and theft of mining land', *National Union Gleanings,* March 1898, Index.

81 'Daily Mail, Feb. 22nd 1898', *National Union Gleanings*, 'The Scheme Explained', March 1898.

82 The first inclusion of an *Express* cutting was in July, 1901.

83 'Daily Express, June 18th 1901', *National Union Gleanings*, 'A Few Press Opinions', July 1901.

84 'Daily Mail and Daily Express, 3 May 1907', *National Union Gleanings*, 'The Radical Exportation of State Secrets', June 1907.

85 'Daily Mail, Jan. 27th 1908', *National Union Gleanings*, 'How Socialists would deal with the Unemployed', February 1908.

86 'Daily Express, Dec. 27th 1907', *National Union Gleanings*, 'How to Fight Socialism', January 1908.

87 The Daily Express on the employment of Chinese Labour in the British Navy', *National Union Gleanings*, August 1907, Index.

88 The notable exception was a verbatim reprint of a *Daily Mail* investigation of the pro-Liberal Cobden Club (Nov. 29th, 1902).

89 'The Alien who Emigrates to England', *National Union Gleanings*, March 1905.

90 Letter from Andrew Bonar Law to Ralph Blumenfeld, 16 November 1910, Blumenfeld papers, Parliamentary Archives [BLU/1/13/LAW.1].

91 Letter from Andrew Bonar Law to Ralph Blumenfeld, 13 January 1912, Blumenfeld papers, Parliamentary Archives [BLU/1/13/LAW.2].

92 Letter from Lord Northcliffe to Lord Beaverbrook, December 1911–January 1913, Beaverbrook Papers, Parliamentary Archives [BBK/G/4/82].

5   Conclusion

What this book has explored, both through its newspaper analyses and its exploration of various party-political archives, represents a significant period of history within British politics and the British press. This period of history saw the rise and consolidation of a new daily mass press which, as Chapters 2 and 3 detailed, represented election news in ways that helped place politics firmly within mass-popular culture, and thus within many of the lived experiences of an imagined 'man in the street'. Elections were reported as dramatic, accessible aspects of day-to-day experiences, in ways that heightened both the power of an archetypal, mass lower-middle-class voter and made political information into digestible, engaging content consumed by millions. Through this, the new dailies were a vibrant and hugely significant addition to this political culture; they were a potent and multi-faceted new form of mass political communication that, as this book has emphasised, spoke particularly to much the same imagined 'man in the street' sought across the Long Edwardian political spectrum.

The political importance of the new dailies must, however, be understood within a critical context. Their success as part of this era's political culture came at the expense of those excluded through their particular vision of mass democracy. On the one hand, the new dailies communicated elections within the framework of broadly socially conservative consumerism. For example, their coverage collectively framed the political sphere as a space where 'rowdyism' was not welcome, as was noted in Chapter 3. Moreover, the intersections between the new dailies' election content and aspects of consumer culture-situated politics very much within aspects of middle-class urban society: the theatre, restaurants, and the music hall – whilst hugely popular – were not political-radical spaces. Their shared articulation of urban elections, therefore, were intrinsically tied to notions of social

DOI: 10.4324/9781003254263-5

respectability, and rarely challenged an electoral culture that excluded many more than it included.

Something this book has particularly noted is the complex place of women within the 'everyman' emphasis both of the new dailies and of wider Long Edwardian election politics. However masculine elections of this period were, it would be disingenuous to argue that women were not involved within them. Indeed, when looking that companies which advertised across all three new dailies, you see a perception that women had a considerable presence within these four general elections. Through an analysis of advertisements, this book has noted how many advertisers pitched their products through a range of often-nuanced political references, sometimes explicitly to readers imagined to be women. Simply put, companies would not have wanted to waste their new daily advertising on an unreceptive audience. The inference being, therefore, that many companies within the mass consumer culture of the period were keenly aware of women's places within general elections, and assumed their election intelligence and agency in their efforts to pitch their variety of products.

This nuance however is absent from the new dailies' news content. Whatever their advertisers may have felt, the new dailies representations of Long Edwardian elections had almost no room for an equivalent 'women in the street'. The few isolated news items explored in this books' four time-period case studies limited and side-lined the role of women within elections: they were portrayed in ways that re-inforced and propagated gendered notions of femininity, in ways that made election interactions very much a man's domain. The limitations placed on women's electoral presence were juxtaposed by the variety of ways in which the 'man in the street' were given agency and significance, as explored in Chapter 3.

The result was a mass press whose iteration of 'mass' politics came with significant limitations. These limitations, however, overlapped with many of the broader limitations of the Long Edwardian franchise. The result was a press whose particular appeal to a 'man in the street' still made them hugely significant during this period, as it was this same 'man in the street' who was of considerable interest to political parties of the period. Chapter 4 study of reactions to this new press from within the three major parties of the period painted a complex picture. It was within Labour that the most diverse and populous reactions were sourced, culminating in their efforts to launch their own party-loyal new daily: the *Citizen*. This short-lived experience was the most visceral evidence of the new daily's impact on the political parties of the Long Edwardian era; it showed a keen awareness of this press's particular appeal to potential lower-middle and working-class voters, and of the broader potential of a mass daily newspaper as a form of political communication.

This book does not claim to be an exhaustive study of this press and its relationship with political culture. Its decision to focus on general elections, for example, offers a chance for further study to delve into this press's broader representations of political news within the Long Edwardian era. Of particular interest would be extent to which the 'man in the street' held significance outside of the particularly masculine sphere of general elections, and whether the gendering of election news was any different outside of these periods. Moreover, the expansion of the franchise after 1918 offers a fascinating opportunity for scholars to explore whether this mass press continued to evolve: did, for example, its election-time coverage change to reflect this changed place of women within the political process, or did the idealised 'man in the street' continue to be reinforced as the dominant force within mass election culture?

Moreover, a wider study of political reactions could offer additional layers to the analyses presented in this book. A variety of additional archives, the selection of additional local collections outside of this book's national emphasis, or those of additional political movements could add much-needed and valuable insight into the ways in which this new press impressed itself onto the political culture of Long Edwardian Britain. What this book has achieved, however, is assert the political significance of the new dailies *Mail, Express*, and *Mirror* within a time period where they were among the most-read newspapers in British history up to that point. Their success came from their appeal to and as part of a wider mass culture that, as scholarship explored in Chapter 1 asserts, was a significant part of political culture. By exploring the ways in which these newspapers – overlooked by much of that past scholarship – were a mass-consumed and dominant part of Long Edwardian general elections, this book corrects this oversight, and hopefully provokes future critical exploration of a newspaper press that was, and continues to be, a significant and controversial form of mass political communication in Britain.

Tables

Table 1 Number of articles featuring the words 'war' AND 'election', separated by newspaper and by general election period

	Daily Mail	Daily Express	Daily Mirror
1900	57	108	N/A
1906	16	47	29
1910 (January)	21	46	10
1910 (December)	14	30	5

Table 2 Number of articles featuring the words 'election' AND 'fight' OR 'fighting', separated by newspaper and by general election period

	Daily Mail	Daily Express	Daily Mirror
1900	104	102	N/A
1906	44	49	43
1910 (January)	42	59	14
1910 (December)	39	40	16

Primary Material

Newspapers & Periodicals

Cooperative News
Daily Citizen
Daily Express
Daily Mail
Daily Mirror
Daily News
Labour Leader
National Union Gleanings

Archive Collections

Bishopsgate Institute, London
Bodleian Library, University of Oxford – Conservative Party Archives
Bristol University Library
British Library, London
London School of Economics – Liberal Special Collections
Parliamentary Archives, London
People's History Museum, Manchester – Labour Party Archives
Working Class Movement Library, Salford

Bibliography

Allen, Joan, and Owen R. Ashton. *Papers for the People : A Study of the Chartist Press*. London: Merlin Press, 2005.

Altick, Richard D. (Richard Daniel). *The English Common Reader : A Social History of the Mass Reading Public, 1800–1900*. Columbus: Ohio State University Press, 1998.

———. *The Shows of London*. Cambridge, MA: Harvard University Press, 1978.

———. *Victorian Studies in Scarlet: Murders and Manners in the Age of Victoria*. New York: W. W. Norton & Company, 1970.

Anwer, Megha. 'Murder in Black and White: Victorian Crime Scenes and the Ripper Photographs'. *Victorian Studies* 56, no. 3 (2014): 433–41. https://doi.org/10.2979/victorianstudies.56.3.433.

Arnold, Matthew. 'Up to Easter'. *The Nineteenth Century No. CXXIII*, May 1887.

Attwood, Rachael Claire. 'Vice beyond the Pale: Representing "white Slavery" in Britain, c.1880–1912'. Doctoral Thesis, UCL (University College London), 2013.

Beers, Laura. *Your Britain : Media and the Making of the Labour Party*. Cambridge, MA: Harvard University Press, 2010.

Bingham, Adrian, and Martin Conboy. *Tabloid Century : The Popular Press in Britain, 1896 to the Present*. Oxford: Peter Lang, 2015.

Blackburn, Robert. *The Electoral System in Britain*. Basingstoke: Macmillan, 1995.

Blaxill, Luke. 'Electioneering, the Third Reform Act, and Political Change in the 1880s*'. *Parliamentary History* 30, no. 3 (October 2011): 343–73. https://doi.org/10.1111/j.1750-0206.2011.00274.x.

———. 'Joseph Chamberlain and the Third Reform Act: A Reassessment of the "Unauthorized Programme" of 1885'. *Journal of British Studies* 54, no. 1 (16 January 2015): 88–117. https://doi.org/10.1017/jbr.2014.251.

———. 'The Language of Imperialism in British Electoral Politics, 1880–1910'. *The Journal of Imperial and Commonwealth History* 45, no. 3 (4 May 2017): 416–48. https://doi.org/10.1080/03086534.2017.1302118.

———. *The War of Words: The Language of British Elections, 1880–1914.* Woodbridge: Boydell & Brewer, 2020.

Boyce, George, James Curran, and Pauline Wingate. *Newspaper History from the Seventeenth Century to the Present Day.* Published for the Press Group of the Acton Society [by] Constable, 1978.

Boyle, Raymond, and Richard Haynes. *Power Play: Sport, the Media and Popular Culture.* Edinburgh: Edinburgh University Press, 2009.

Bratton, Jacky. *The Making of the West End Stage: Marriage, Management and the Mapping of Gender in London, 1830–1870.* Cambridge: Cambridge University Press, 2011.

Breton, Rob. 'Crime Reporting in Chartist Newspapers'. *Media History* 19, no. 3 (August 2013): 244–56. https://doi.org/10.1080/13688804.2013.820104.

Brodie, Marc. 'Voting in the Victorian and Edwardian East End of London'. *Parliamentary History* 23, no. 2 (17 March 2004): 225–48. https://doi.org/10.1111/j.1750-0206.2004.tb00728.x.

Brown, Lucy. *Victorian News and Newspapers.* Oxford: Clarendon Press, 1985.

Campbell, Kate. 'W. E. Gladstone, W. T. Stead, Matthew Arnold and a New Journalism: Cultural Politics in the 1880s'. *Victorian Periodicals Review* 36, no. 1 (2003): 20–40.

Casey, Christopher A. 'Common Misperceptions: The Press and Victorian Views of Crime'. *Journal of Interdisciplinary History* 41, no. 3 (December 2010): 367–91. https://doi.org/10.1162/JINH_a_00106.

Casson, Mark. *The World's First Railway System : Enterprise, Competition, and Regulation on the Railway Network in Victorian Britain.* Oxford: Oxford University Press, 2009.

Chovanec, Jan. '"…But There Were No Broken Legs"'. *Journal of Historical Pragmatics* 15, no. 2 (2014): 228–54. https://doi.org/10.1075/jhp.15.2.05cho.

Conboy, Martin. *The Press and Popular Culture.* London: SAGE, 2002.

Cranfield, Geoffrey. *The Press and Society: From Caxton to Northcliffe.* London: Longman, 1978.

Curtis, L. Perry. *Jack the Ripper and the London Press.* New Haven, CT: Yale University Press, 2001.

Davis, John. 'The Enfranchisement of the Urban Poor in Late-Victorian Britain'. In *Politics and Culture in Victorian Britain*, edited by Peter Ghosh, Lawrence Goldman, and Colin Matthew, 95–117. Oxford: Oxford University Press, 2006. https://doi.org/10.1093/acprof:oso/9780199253456.003.0007.

Ensor, R. C. K. (Robert Charles Kirkwood). *England, 1870–1914.* Oxford: Clarendon Press, 1936.

Epstein, James. 'Feargus O'Connor and the Northern Star'. *International Review of Social History* 21, no. 1 (18 April 1976): 51–97. https://doi.org/10.1017/S0020859000005137.

Epstein, James. *The Lion of Freedom : Feargus O'Connor and the Chartist Movement, 1832–1842.* London: Croom Helm, 1982.

Franklin, Bob. *Packaging Politics: Political Communications in Britain's Media Democracy.* London: Edward Arnold, 1994.

Fraser, Derek. *Urban Politics in Victorian England : The Structure of Politics in Victorian Cities.* Leicester: Leicester University Press, 1976.

Freeman, Michael J. *Railways and the Victorian Imagination*. New Haven, CT: Yale University Press, 1999.

Gorham, Deborah. 'The "Maiden Tribute of Modern Babylon" Re-examined: Child Prostitution and the Idea of Childhood in Late-Victorian England'. *Victorian Studies* 21, no. 3 (1978): 353–79. https://doi.org/10.2307/3827386.

Griffiths, Dennis. *Fleet Street: Five Hundred Years of the Press*. London: British Library, 2006.

Grossman, Jonathan H. *Charles Dickens's Networks: Public Transport and the Novel*. Oxford: Oxford University Press, 2012.

Gurney, Peter. *The Making of Consumer Culture in Modern Britain*. London: Bloomsbury Academic, 2017.

Hampton, Mark. 'Liberalism, the Press, and the Construction of the Public Sphere: Theories of the Press in Britain, 1830–1914'. *Victorian Periodicals Review* 37, no. 1 (2004): 72–92. https://doi.org/10.2307/20083990.

———. '"Understanding Media": Theories of the Press in Britain, 1850–1914'. *Media, Culture & Society* 23, no. 2 (30 March 2001): 213–31. https://doi.org/10.1177/016344301023002004.

Harrison, Stanley. *Poor Men's Guardians: A Record of the Struggles for a Democratic Newspaper Press, 1763–1973*. London: Lawrence and Wishart, 1974.

Hewitt, Martin. *The Dawn of the Cheap Press in Victorian Britain: The End of the 'Taxes on Knowledge', 1849–1869*. London: Bloomsbury, 2014.

Hollis, Patricia. *The Pauper Press: A Study in Working-Class Radicalism of the 1830s*. Oxford: Oxford University Press, 1970.

Holt, Richard. *Sport and the British: A Modern History*. Oxford: Oxford University Press, 1990.

Hopkins, Deian. 'The Socialist Press in Britain, 1890–1910'. In *Newspaper History from the Seventeenth Century to the Present Day*, edited by James Curran, George Boyce, and Pauline Wingate, 265–80. London: Sage/Constable, 1978.

Horrall, Andrew. *Popular Culture in London c. 1890–1918: The Transformation of Entertainment*. Manchester: Manchester University Press, 2001.

Hughes, Michael, and Harry Wood. 'Crimson Nightmares: Tales of Invasion and Fears of Revolution in Early Twentieth-Century Britain'. *Contemporary British History* 28, no. 3 (3 July 2014): 294–317. https://doi.org/10.1080/13619462.2014.941817.

Jacobs, Edward. 'Edward Lloyd's Sunday Newspapers and the Cultural Politics of Crime News, c. 1840–43'. *Victorian Periodicals Review* 50, no. 3 (2017): 619–49. https://doi.org/10.1353/vpr.2017.0043.

Jenkins, Terence Andrew. 'Political Life in Late Victorian Britain: The Conservatives in Thornbury'. *Parliamentary History* 23, no. 2 (17 March 2004): 198–224. https://doi.org/10.1111/j.1750-0206.2004.tb00727.x.

Johnson, Ray. 'Tricks, Traps, and Transformations'. *Early Popular Visual Culture* 5, no. 2 (2007): 151–65. https://doi.org/10.1080/17460650701433673.

Johnston, Neil. 'The History of the Parliamentary Franchise'. London: House of Commons Library, 2013.

Jones, Aled. *Powers of the Press: Newspapers, Power and the Public in Nineteenth-Century England*. Aldershot: Scolar Press, 1996.

Knelman, Judith. 'Subtly Sensational: A Study of Early Victorian Crime Reporting'. *Journal of Newspaper and Periodical History* 8, no. 1 (1992): 34–41.
———. *Twisting in the Wind: The Murderess and the English Press*. Toronto: University of Toronto Press, 1998. https://doi.org/10.3138/9781442682818.
Koss, Stephen E. *The Rise and Fall of the Political Press in Britain*. London: Hamish Hamilton, 1984.
Law, Graham, and Matthew Sterenberg. 'Old v. New Journalism and the Public Sphere; or, Habermas Encounters Dallas and Stead'. *19: Interdisciplinary Studies in the Long Nineteenth Century* 1, no. 16 (22 March 2013). https://doi.org/10.16995/ntn.657.
Lawrence, Jon. *Electing Our Masters: The Hustings in British Politics from Hogarth to Blair*. Oxford: Oxford University Press, 2009.
———. *Speaking for the People: Party, Language and Popular Politics in England, 1867–1914*. Cambridge: Cambridge University Press, 1998.
Lee, Alan J. *The Origins of the Popular Press in England, 1855–1914*. London: Croom Helm, 1976.
Lewis, Rob. '"Our Lady Specialists at Pikes Lane": Female Spectators in Early English Professional Football, 1880–1914'. *The International Journal of the History of Sport* 26, no. 15 (December 2009): 2161–81. https://doi.org/10.1080/09523360903367651.
Lightman, Bernard. 'Victorian Science and Popular Visual Culture'. *Early Popular Visual Culture* 10, no. 1 (2012): 1–5. https://doi.org/10.1080/17460654.2012.637389.
Lodge, David. *Consciousness and the Novel: Connected Essays*. Cambridge, MA: Harvard University Press, 2002.
Malone, Carolyn. 'Campaigning Journalism: The Clarion, the Daily Citizen, and the Protection of Women Workers, 1898–1912'. *Labour History Review* 67, no. 3 (2002): 281–97.
Marsh, Peter. *Joseph Chamberlain: Entrepreneur in Politics*. New Haven, CT: Yale University Press, 1994.
Mason, Tony. *Association Football and English Society, 1863–1915*. Brighton: Harvester Press, 1980.
———. 'Sporting News, 1860–1914'. In *The Press in English Society from the Seventeenth to the Nineteenth Centuries*, edited by Michael Harris and Alan Lee. London/Toronto: Associated University Presses, 1986.
Matthew, Colin. 'Rhetoric and Politics in Great Britain 1860–1950'. In *Politics and Social Change in Modern Britain*, edited by Philip John Waller. Brighton: Harvester Press, 1987.
McEwen, John M. 'Lloyd George's Acquisition of the Daily Chronicle in 1918'. *Journal of British Studies* 22, no. 1 (1982): 127–44. https://doi.org/10.2307/175660.
McIntire, Matthew. 'Odds, Intelligence, and Prophecies: Racing News in the Penny Press, 1855–1914'. *Victorian Periodicals Review* 41, no. 4 (2008): 352–73. https://doi.org/10.1353/vpr.0.0056.
McKibbin, Ross. 'Why Was There No Marxism in Great Britain?' *English Historical Review* 49 (1984): 297–331.

McWilliam, Rohan. *London's West End: Creating the Pleasure District, 1800–1914. London's West End*. Oxford: Oxford University Press, 2020.

Miller, Henry. 'The 1910 Petitions on Women's Suffrage: An Unofficial Referendum-Committees-UKParliament'. UKParliamentCommittees,2017. https://committees.parliament.uk/committee/326/petitions-committee/news/99171/the-1910-petitions-on-womens-suffrage-an-unofficial-referendum/.

Mussell, James. '"Characters of Blood and Flame": Stead and the Tabloid Campaign'. In *W. T. Stead: Newspaper Revolutionary*, edited by Laurel Brake, Ed King, James Mussell, and Roger Luckhurst, 22–36. London: British Library, 2012.

Nord, David Paul. 'The Victorian City and the Urban Newspaper'. In *Making News: The Political Economy of Journalism in Britain and America from the Glorious Revolution to the Internet*, edited by Richard R. John and Jonathan Silberstein-Loeb, 73–106. Oxford: Oxford University Press, 2015.

Otter, Chris. *The Victorian Eye: A Political History of Light and Vision in Britain, 1800–1910*. Chicago: University of Chicago Press, 2008.

Parratt, Catriona M. 'Little Means or Time: Working–Class Women and Leisure in Late Victorian and Edwardian England'. *International Journal of Phytoremediation* 21, no. 1 (1998): 22–53. https://doi.org/10.1080/09523369808714027.

Pickering, Paul A. *Feargus O'Connor: A Political Life*. London: Merlin Press, 2008.

Plowden, William. *The Motor Car and Politics in Britain*. Harmondsworth: Penguin, 1973.

Potter, Simon J. 'Jingoism, Public Opinion, and the New Imperialism'. *Media History* 20, no. 1 (2 January 2014): 34–50. https://doi.org/10.1080/13688804.2013.869067.

Pugh, Martin. *The Making of Modern British Politics, 1867–1945*. London: Blackwells, 2002.

Rains, Stephanie. 'Going in for Competitions'. *Media History* 21, no. 2 (3 April 2015): 138–49. https://doi.org/10.1080/13688804.2014.995611.

Rappaport, Erika. *Shopping for Pleasure: Women in the Making of London's West End*. Princeton, NJ: Princeton University Press, 2001.

Read, Donald. *The Age of Urban Democracy : England 1868–1914*. 2nd ed. London: Routledge, 1994.

Readman, Paul. 'The 1895 General Election and Political Change in Late Victorian Britain'. *The Historical Journal* 42, no. 2 (1999): 467–93.

———. 'The Conservative Party, Patriotism, and British Politics: The Case of the General Election of 1900'. *Journal of British Studies* 40, no. 1 (2001): 107–45. https://doi.org/10.2307/3070771.

Richardson, Sarah. 'Parliament as Viewed Through a Woman's Eyes: Gender and Space in the 19th-Century Commons'. *Parliamentary History* 38, no. 1 (1 February 2019): 119–34. https://doi.org/10.1111/1750-0206.12416.

Rix, Kathryn. '"The Elimination of Corrupt Practices in British Elections"? Reassessing the Impact of the 1883 Corrupt Practices Act'. *The English*

Historical Review CXXIII, no. 500 (1 February 2008): 65–97. https://doi. org/10.1093/EHR/CEN005.

Roberts, Matthew. *Political Movements in Urban England, 1832–1914*. Basingstoke: Palgrave Macmillan, 2009.

———. 'Resisting "Arithmocracy": Parliament, Community, and the Third Reform Act'. *The Journal of British Studies* 50, no. 2 (21 April 2011): 381–409. https://doi.org/10.1086/658188.

Robson, Ann. 'The Significance of "The Maiden Tribute of Modern Babylon"'. *Victorian Periodicals Newsletter* 11, no. 2 (1978): 50–57. https://doi. org/10.2307/20085183.

Samples, Jonathan. 'Working-Class Prose: The "Northern Star" and Radical Discourse during the First-Wave of the Chartist Movement - ProQuest'. Master Thesis (Roosevelt University), 2013.

Sanderson, Michael. 'Literacy and Social Mobility in the Industrial Revolution in England'. *Past and Present* 56, no. 1 (1972): 75–103. https://doi. org/10.1093/past/56.1.75.

Schneer, Jonathan. *London 1900: The Imperial Metropolis*. New Haven, CT: Yale University Press, 2001.

Shannon, Richard. *The Age of Salisbury, 1881–1902 : Unionism and Empire*. London: Longman, 1996.

Sharpe, Iain. 'Empire, Patriotism and the Working-Class Electorate: The 1900 General Election in the Battersea Constituency'. *Parliamentary History* 28, no. 3 (1 October 2009): 392–412. https://doi. org/10.1111/j.1750-0206.2009.00116.x.

Shoop-Worrall, Christopher. 'Scouse Sensation'. *Media History* 27, no. 2 (2021): 148–61. https://doi.org/10.1080/13688804.2019.1652583.

Stevenson, Jon. *British Social History 1914–45*. Harmondsworth: Penguin, 1984.

Stoddart, Susan. 'Pressing or Reform: The New Liberalism and Emotion in Edwardian Liberal Newspapers'. Doctoral Thesis (Royal Holloway, University of London), 2014.

Stone, Lawrence. 'Literacy and Education in England 1640–1900'. *Past and Present* 42, no. 1 (1969): 69–139. https://doi.org/10.1093/past/42.1.69.

Takayanagi, Mari. 'Women and the Vote: The Parliamentary Path to Equal Franchise, 1918–28'. *Parliamentary History* 37, no. 1 (February 2018): 168–85. https://doi.org/10.1111/1750-0206.12344.

Tholfsen, Trygve R. 'The Transition to Democracy in Victorian England'. *International Review of Social History* 6, no. 2 (18 August 1961): 226–48. https://doi.org/10.1017/S0020859000001838.

Thomas, John Alun. *The House of Commons 1906–1911*. Cardiff: University of Wales Press, 1958.

Thompson, James. *British Political Culture and the Idea of 'Public Opinion', 1867–1914*. Cambridge: Cambridge University Press, 2013.

———. '"Pictorial Lies"? - Posters and Politics in Britain c.1880–1914'. *Past and Present* 197, no. 1 (2007): 177–210. https://doi.org/10.1093/pastj/gtm051.

————. "'The Lights of the Electric Octopus Have Been Switched Off'": Visual and Political Culture in Edwardian London'. *Twentieth Century British History*, 13 December 2017. https://doi.org/10.1093/tcbh/hwx062.

Thorpe, Andrew. *A History of the British Labour Party*. 3rd ed. Basingstoke: Palgrave Macmillan, 2008.

Vamplew, Wray. *Pay Up and Play the Game: Professional Sport in Britain, 1875–1914*. Cambridge: Cambridge University Press, 1988.

Vessey, David. 'Words as Well as Deeds: The Popular Press and Suffragette Hunger Strikes in Edwardian Britain'. *Twentieth Century British History* 32, no. 1 (7 August 2021): 68–92. https://doi.org/10.1093/tcbh/hwaa031.

Walker, Lynn. 'Vistas of Pleasure: Women Consumers and Urban Space in the West End of London, 1850–1900'. In *Women in the Victorian Art World*, edited by Clarissa Campbell Orr, 70–88. Manchester: Manchester University Press, 1995.

Walton, John K. *The British Seaside : Holidays and Resorts in the Twentieth Century*. Manchester: Manchester University Press, 2000.

Waters, Chris. *British Socialists and the Politics of Popular Culture, 1884–1914*. Manchester: Manchester University Press, 1990.

Webb, Robert K. 'Working Class Readers in Early Victorian England'. *The English Historical Review* LXV, no. CCLVI (1 July 1950): 333–51. https://doi.org/10.1093/ehr/LXV.CCLVI.333.

Wendelin, Greta. 'A Rhetoric of Pornography: Private Style and Public Policy in "The Maiden Tribute of Modern Babylon"'. *Rhetoric Society Quarterly* 42, no. 4 (July 2012): 375–96. https://doi.org/10.1080/02773945.2012.704120.

Wiener, Joel H. *Papers for the Millions : The New Journalism in Britain, 1850s to 1914*. New York: Greenwood Press, 1988.

————. *The Americanization of the British Press, 1830s-1914 : Speed in the Age of Transatlantic Journalism*. Basingstoke: Palgrave Macmillan, 2011.

————. *The War of the Unstamped : The Movement to Repeal the British Newspaper Tax, 1830–1836*. Ithaca, NY: Cornell University Press, 1969.

Wilkinson, Gavin. "'The Blessings of War'": The Depiction of Military Force in Edwardian Newspapers'. *Journal of Contemporary History* 33, no. 1 (1998): 97–115.

Williams, Jean. *A Game for Rough Girls? A History of Women's Football in Britain*. London: Routledge, 2003.

Williams, Kevin. *Read All About It! A History of the British Newspaper*. London: Routledge, 2010.

Wilson, Andrew Norman. *The Victorians*. New York: Arrow, 2003.

Windscheffel, Alex. *Popular Conservatism in Imperial London, 1868–1906*. London: Royal Historical Society, 2007.

Yan, Shu-chuan. 'Emotions, Sensations, and Victorian Working-Class Readers'. *The Journal of Popular Culture* 50, no. 2 (April 2017): 317–40. https://doi.org/10.1111/jpcu.12535.

Index

For Product Safety Concerns and Information please contact our EU
representative GPSR@taylorandfrancis.com Taylor & Francis Verlag GmbH,
Kaufingerstraße 24, 80331 München, Germany

Printed and bound by CPI Group (UK) Ltd, Croydon, CR0 4YY
11/04/2025
01844011-0005